Applied Ethics in Student Services

Harry J. Canon, Robert D. Brown, *Editors*

NEW DIRECTIONS FOR STUDENT SERVICES
URSULA DELWORTH, GARY R. HANSON, *Editors-in-Chief*
Number 30, June 1985

Paperback sourcebooks in
The Jossey-Bass Higher Education Series

Jossey-Bass Inc., Publishers
San Francisco • Washington • London

Harry J. Canon, Robert D. Brown (Eds.).
Applied Ethics in Student Services.
New Directions for Student Services, no. 30.
San Francisco: Jossey-Bass, 1985.

New Directions for Student Services Series
Ursula Delworth and Gary R. Hanson, *Editors-in-Chief*

Copyright © 1985 by Jossey-Bass Inc., Publishers
and
Jossey-Bass Limited

Copyright under International, Pan American, and Universal Copyright Conventions. All rights reserved. No part of this issue may be reproduced in any form — except for brief quotation (not to exceed 500 words) in a review or professional work — without permission in writing from the publishers.

New Directions for Student Services (publication number USPS 449-070) is published quarterly by Jossey-Bass Inc., Publishers. Second-class postage rates paid at San Francisco, California, and at additional mailing offices.

Correspondence:
Subscriptions, single-issue orders, change of address notices, undelivered copies, and other correspondence should be sent to Subscriptions, Jossey-Bass Inc., Publishers, 433 California Street, San Francisco, California 94104.

Editorial correspondence should be sent to the Editors-in-Chief, Ursula Delworth, University Counseling Service, Iowa Memorial Union, University of Iowa, Iowa City, Iowa 52242 or Gary R. Hanson, Office of the Dean of Students, Student Services Building, Room 101, University of Texas at Austin, Austin, Texas 78712.

Library of Congress Catalogue Card Number LC 84-82379
International Standard Serial Number ISSN 0164-7970
International Standard Book Number ISBN 87589-768-1

Cover art by Willi Baum
Manufactured in the United States of America

Ordering Information

The paperback sourcebooks listed below are published quarterly and can be ordered either by subscription or single-copy.

Subscriptions cost $35.00 per year for institutions, agencies, and libraries. Individuals can subscribe at the special rate of $25.00 per year *if payment is by personal check*. (Note that the full rate of $35.00 applies if payment is by institutional check, even if the subscription is designated for an individual.) Standing orders are accepted. Subscriptions normally begin with the first of the four sourcebooks in the current publication year of the series. When ordering, please indicate if you prefer your subscription to begin with the first issue of the *coming* year.

Single copies are available at $8.95 when payment accompanies order, and *all single-copy orders under $25.00 must include payment*. (California, New Jersey, New York, and Washington, D.C., residents please include appropriate sales tax.) For billed orders, cost per copy is $8.95 plus postage and handling. (Prices subject to change without notice.)

Bulk orders (ten or more copies) of any individual sourcebook are available at the following discounted prices: 10–49 copies, $8.05 each; 50–100 copies, $7.15 each; over 100 copies, *inquire*. Sales tax and postage and handling charges apply as for single copy orders.

To ensure correct and prompt delivery, all orders must give either the *name of an individual* or an *official purchase order number*. Please submit your order as follows:

Subscriptions: specify series and year subscription is to begin.
Single Copies: specify sourcebook code (such as, SS8) and first two words of title.

Mail orders for United States and Possessions, Latin America, Canada, Japan, Australia, and New Zealand to:
 Jossey-Bass Inc., Publishers
 433 California Street
 San Francisco, California 94104

Mail orders for all other parts of the world to:
 Jossey-Bass Limited
 28 Banner Street
 London EC1Y 8QE

New Directions for Student Services Series
Ursula Delworth, Gary R. Hanson, *Editors-in-Chief*

SS1 *Evaluating Program Effectiveness,* Gary R. Hanson
SS2 *Training Competent Staff,* Ursula Delworth
SS3 *Reducing the Dropout Rate,* Lee Noel
SS4 *Applying New Developmental Findings,* Lee Knefelkamp, Carole Widick, Clyde A. Parker

SS5 *Consulting on Campus,* M. Kathryn Hamilton, Charles J. Meade
SS6 *Utilizing Futures Research,* Frederick R. Brodzinski
SS7 *Establishing Effective Programs,* Margaret J. Barr, Lou Ann Keating
SS8 *Redesigning Campus Environments,* Lois Huebner
SS9 *Applying Management Techniques,* Cecelia H. Foxley
SS10 *Serving Handicapped Students,* Hazel Z. Sprandel, Marlin R. Schmidt
SS11 *Providing Student Services for the Adult Learner,* Arthur Shriberg
SS12 *Responding to Changes in Financial Aid Programs,* Shirley F. Binder
SS13 *Increasing the Educational Role of Residence Halls,* Gregory S. Blimling, John H. Schuh
SS14 *Facilitating Students' Career Development,* Vincent A. Harren, M. Harry Daniels, Jacqueline N. Buck
SS15 *Education for Student Development,* Jane Fried
SS16 *Understanding Today's Students,* David DeCoster, Phyllis Mable
SS17 *Developmental Approaches to Academic Advising,* Roger Winston, Jr., Steven Ender, Theodore Miller
SS18 *Helping the Learning Disabled Student,* Marlin R. Schmidt, Hazel Z. Sprandel
SS19 *Mentoring-Transcript Systems for Promoting Student Growth,* Robert D. Brown, David A. DeCoster
SS20 *Measuring Student Development,* Gary R. Hanson
SS21 *Helping Students Manage Stress,* Elizabeth M. Altmaier
SS22 *Student Affairs and the Law,* Margaret J. Barr
SS23 *Understanding Student Affairs Organizations,* George D. Kuh
SS24 *Commuter Students: Enhancing Their Educational Potential,* Sylvia S. Stewart
SS25 *Orienting Students to College,* M. Lee Upcraft
SS26 *Enhancing Student Development with Computers,* Cynthia S. Johnson, K. Richard Pyle
SS27 *Using Students as Paraprofessional Staff,* Steven C. Ender, Roger B. Winston
SS28 *Rethinking Services for College Athletes,* Arthur Shriberg, Frederick R. Brodzinski
SS29 *Facilitating the Development of Women,* Nancy J. Evans

Contents

Editors' Notes — 1
Harry J. Canon, Robert D. Brown

Chapter 1. Ethical Problems in Daily Practice — 5
Harry J. Canon
Illustrative cases are presented that suggest the range and scope of ethical issues in student services.

Chapter 2. Ethical Principles and Ethical Decisions in Student Affairs — 17
Karen Strohm Kitchener
Ethical principles can offer critical assistance in sorting out conflicts among various ethical code provisions and provide for rational decision making.

Chapter 3. A New Model for Defining Ethical Behavior — 31
LuAnn Krager
A schematic format is provided that enables the defining of specific behavioral expectations drawn from both professional roles and ethical principles.

Chapter 4. Ethical Standards Statements: Uses and Limitations — 49
Roger B. Winston, Jr., John C. Dagley
Several ethical codes of student services professional organizations are examined and their biases and limitations described.

Chapter 5. Creating an Ethical Community — 67
Robert D. Brown
The importance of developing and utilizing a community in support of the achievement of ethical ideals is illustrated.

Chapter 6. How to Think About Professional Ethics — 81
Harry J. Canon, Robert D. Brown
Some commonly held beliefs about ethics and the relevance of an ethics of care is described.

Appendixes — 89
This reference section contains the ethical codes of the American College Personnel Association and the National Association of Student Personnel Administrators.

Index — 103

Editors' Notes

It is the first day of freshman orientation at Central State. Several hundred new students are assembled in a lecture hall to be welcomed by State's dean of undergraduate instruction. The dean looks up from the podium and says, "I want you to look at the person on your right and at the person on your left. One of the three of you will not be here next fall."

New students have heard this threadbare academic cliché for as long as most of us can remember. It is the first in a series of ethical issues that provide the raw material for this sourcebook. Readers who are already familiar with the ethical codes of the major student services professional organizations will recognize that Central State's dean of instruction has violated none of those codes. At the same time, those familiar with the exploration of ethical systems and principles will note that the dean's opening statement has the potential for violating certain ethical principles. Many of us are made uneasy by the application of strategies designed to intimidate rather than to support; we may conclude that the dean's statement is not unethical but that it is bad student personnel practice. Bad student personnel practice is a common by-product of substandard ethical practice. We will review this and other cases in this sourcebook with the goal of understanding the qualities of high ethical standards and the means for achieving them.

It is our intent to encourage examination of the ethical quality of practices in the student services professions, to use professional ethical codes as reference points, to understand how individual codes differ from one another and why those differences may have arisen, to explore the application of ethical principles to ethical decision making, to apply some role definitions and see how their descriptors affect our meeting of ethical responsibilities to one another, and, in general, to elevate our inquiry into ethical matters to levels above the minima required by laws and our formal codes.

Ethics and Student Development

Two critical assumptions inform the chapters that follow: First, student services are provided in the context of facilitating the intellectual and personal growth of our student clientele. Second, the maintenance of an ethical climate is a necessary precondition for accomplishment of developmental tasks. The second assumption is an admittedly untested elaboration of Nevitt Sanford's (1979, p. 110) identification of "challenge and support" as the necessary and possibly sufficient conditions for growth and change. It seems to us that a commonsense definition of support would of necessity assume an environment that the individual perceives as ethical (Canon, 1983). To put the matter another way, it is difficult to feel supported in an environment characterized by the absence of fairness, honesty, and justice. Maintenance of an ethical climate becomes essential if we are to assist students in the accomplishment of their developmental tasks.

Some Barriers to Ethical Inquiry

There is every reason to assume that student services professionals wish to conduct themselves in an ethically acceptable manner. It is probable that most of us behave in ethically commendable ways as we carry out our day-to-day professional responsibilities. Nonetheless, many of us seem to be uncomfortable as we undertake the real-life exploration of ethical matters with our colleagues. Some dimensions of that discomfort need to be acknowledged at this early point if we are to deal effectively with the concepts and issues that follow.

An ethics task force composed of a portion of the American College Personnel Association (ACPA) leadership met in St. Louis in the fall of 1983 (Johnson, 1983). It concluded that the few convention programs of the past several years that had dealt with ethical issues had been poorly attended, although the presenters and panelists ordinarily could be expected to draw substantial audiences. It was noted that the major student services journals received few articles dealing with ethical issues. A few participants recalled that hearings convened for the purpose of amending the proposed ethical code had been attended by no more than two or three individuals, although some code statements were thought to be highly controversial. Much of the task force discussion focused on the perception that our professional organizations seemed to have difficulty in creating a climate in which members could discuss and argue ethical issues comfortably.

Several circumstances may contribute to that apparent discomfort. We have barely begun to emerge from the era in which in loco parentis precepts were abandoned. We have commented elsewhere (Brown and Canon, 1978) about the void thus created. Having conceded that they were no longer the moral arbiters of student behavior, student affairs professionals began to create quasi-legal systems and codes and tentatively concluded that matters of student ethics and morals were no longer within their purview. The pendulum is only now beginning to swing back from an extreme that seemingly endorsed (or at a minimum ignored) any mode of student self-indulgence that did not immediately and negatively affect the welfare of others. We have been most reluctant to raise issues of morality or ethics with student constituents for fear of seeming self-righteous. During the same period, just what the normative ethical behaviors might be for faculty and staff—including student services staff—became increasingly uncertain. *Moral turpitude,* that old standby from faculty and staff contracts, ceased to have useful meaning. In general, the climate on most of our campuses was one of tolerance for increasingly distant ethical and moral boundaries. Any challenge to increased tolerance risked the countercharge of being moralistic.

And so, it appears that our changing mores, both on and off campus, have helped in a substantive way to make ethical issues less "fashionable." Fortunately, there is some evidence that fashion is changing with respect to the exploration of ethical matters. With the support of such agencies as the Hastings Center, courses in applied ethics are beginning to appear in increasing numbers of professional training programs. A public television series dealing with ethical standards in journalism and law has drawn sizable audiences. The popular press regularly features articles on the complexity of ethical issues and ethical decision making in medicine. In short, support for a new focus on ethics seems to be emerging.

Chapter One of this sourcebook offers case studies that touch on a variety of areas of practice in the student services. The case study format was selected because of its potential effectiveness as a teaching medium in addressing ethical concepts. These cases, which other authors in the sourcebook will discuss, can be used for staff or class discussions. The editors are indebted to Jack Donahue, Jane Fried, Donna McKinley, Earl Nolting, Patricia Rissmeyer, John Welty, Doris Wright, and other colleagues who contributed incidents and cases that they believed had potential for illustrating the variety of ethical issues that student services professionals encounter.

In Chapter Two, Karen Kitchener shows how five key ethical principles can have practical use in defining the core issues of an ethics case. She draws on the scholarly literature in ethics to explain in everyday terms why professional codes commonly fall short of helping us to find a "clean" resolution for many ethical dilemmas.

The tabular scheme offered by LuAnn Krager in Chapter Three provides a new and effective means for identifying specific ethical behaviors that student services professionals can adopt if they take the principles suggested by Kitchener seriously. We suspect that many readers will find additional applications for Krager's model as they examine their professional roles in the light of the specified ethical principles.

The shared knowledge and experience of Roger Winston and John Dagley bring to Chapter Four a rich understanding of how ethical codes are constructed and of their particular biases, strengths, and deficiencies. The authors make clear the futility of blind reliance on professional ethical codes to provide "cookbook" answers to real-life ethical dilemmas.

In Chapter Five, we explore the need for the creation of a community that consistently and intentionally concerns itself with the provision of an ethical environment in which we and our students can grow. That this sourcebook ever became a reality is the consequence of just such a community of professional and personal support; Peg Barr, Russ Brown, Ursula Delworth, Jim

Hurst, Cynthia Johnson, Donna McKinley, Marv Moore, Wes Morrill, and Phil Tripp—both individually and as a caring professional community—supported us over a nine-year period when ethical inquiry seemed very much out of fashion. While Chapter Five is "prophetic" in style, we believe that its suggestions have the potential for significantly enhancing the quality of our professional lives and the development of the students who are the reason for our professional existence. In Chapter Six, we suggest that an ethics of care is congruent both with student services philosophy and with the nature of those who are part of the student services professions.

Harry J. Canon
Robert D. Brown
Editors

References

Brown, R. D., and Canon, H. J. "Intentional Moral Development as an Objective of Higher Education." *Journal of College Student Personnel,* 1978, *19,* 426-429

Canon, H. J. "The Ethical Climate and Student Development." Paper presented at the American College Personnel Association convention, Houston, March 15, 1983.

Johnson, D. "Ethics Task Group Summary." Unpublished report to the Executive Committee of the American College Personnel Association, Minneapolis, December, 1983.

Sanford, N. "Freshman Personality: A Stage in Human Development." In N. Sanford and J. Axelrod, Eds. *College and Character.* Berkeley: Montaigne, 1979.

Harry J. Canon is professor of leadership and educational policy studies at Northern Illinois University and current chair of the Professional Ethics and Conduct Committee of the American College Personnel Association.

Robert D. Brown is professor of educational psychology and measurements at the University of Nebraska-Lincoln. The Editor of the Journal of College Student Personnel, *he is the recipient of the American College Personnel Association's Contribution to Knowledge Award.*

Cases drawn from a variety of areas of professional practice in student services raise issues that may or may not be clarified by existing professional ethical codes.

Ethical Problems in Daily Practice

Harry J. Canon

Student affairs professionals function in a variety of arenas and with varied constituencies. Those constituencies include graduate students preparing for student services careers, individual undergraduate and graduate students, student organizations, professional colleagues in student affairs, faculty colleagues, senior administrators, parents, governance structures and bodies, and external constituencies who have an interest in the manner in which we conduct student services in higher education. The arenas include agency offices, public forums, classrooms, residence halls, conferences and conventions, state legislatures, and the institutional boardroom. Each population combines with each setting to yield a nearly unique set of circumstances, and with that set of circumstances can come a unique set of ethical dilemmas to be faced and resolved.

In the case presentations that follow, some readers will find profound ethical issues, other readers will conclude that both the situation and its resolution are obvious, and still others will assert that no ethical problem exists. Readers are encouraged to assess each case against their own background of experiences, values, and perceptions. Somewhat like life itself, this sourcebook offers no ultimate answers. Our objective in sharing these cases is to have the reader join with us in pursuing successive approximations of ethical truths.

All cases are based on real-life experiences, but the details have been disguised. In each instance, a student affairs professional has believed that the case represents or raises a matter of professional ethical concern. The cases are numbered for ease of subsequent reference.

The Preparation of Student Affairs Professionals

The relationship between graduate student and faculty member is delicate and subtle in character. In an enlightened system, the graduate student is increasingly being accorded the status of apprentice colleague. Nonetheless, in this inherently unequal partnership, the faculty member retains awesome power over the student's academic and professional future. Maintenance of professional standards calls for legitimate assertions of control; a faculty member's human failings may lead him or her to misuse that power.

Case 1. Jim is a candidate for a master's degree and elected to do a thesis research project for six of his thirty-six semester hours. His adviser, Professor X, is engaged in a long-term research project dealing with the characteristics of students in the fraternity/sorority system. Jim's basic thesis concept is part of Professor X's larger project. While Jim contributed little to the research design, he did invest more than a thousand hours in the project, not counting the time involved in writing the thesis itself. The results of Jim's portion of the larger investigation seem important enough to warrant a journal article. Professor X indicates his willingness to write and submit the article for publication with a footnote to acknowledge Jim's contribution.

Case 2. A seminar course in group process is part of the core curriculum for all students enrolled in the College Student Personnel program at Alpha University. Besides attending a didactic session of the course each week, the seminar participants meet for an additional two hours to constitute themselves as a "process group." The faculty member who teaches the course explains to the students that being a group member helps participants to gain an appreciation for group process; it may also help them with their "personal growth." Students who have taken the course in other years observe that they have had to walk a fine line between revealing enough of themselves to prevent being labeled "defensive" and at the same time not enough of themselves to be advised that they have "serious personal problems that have to be worked through in therapy" if they are to continue in the graduate program.

Case 3. In the course of a faculty meeting in which the promise of master's students for the doctoral program is being reviewed, it occurs to June that she has been less receptive to some students than to others. As she reflects on her pattern of attending to students, she concludes that she is more likely to "have time to visit" with students who are more articulate, who express interest in her specialty area, and who are physically attractive. She does not share this conclusion with her faculty colleagues but continues to worry about the matter in private moments.

Case 4. A professor supervises the initial practicum course in counseling. Some of the practicum students are made uncomfortable by this instructor's persistent sexual references and jokes; others resent the instructor's habit of touching them on the arm or the shoulder while speaking to them in supervisory sessions. All the students in the practicum section are inclined to view the professor as "essentially harmless" and a rather caring faculty member.

Encounters with Students

One of the most powerful means of affording moral education to students is through the role modeling provided by faculty and professional staff (Bok, 1982; Brubacher, 1982). Decisions to evade a moral issue or to arrive at an accommodation of convenience that is ethically marginal are no less powerful as teaching devices than thoughtful and morally courageous actions are. The student services staff member is often in a position to decide to address or not address an issue that affects a particular student or small group of students. The pressures of the day, reactions from supervisors, and simple fatigue may affect the ethical quality of the decision. Whatever external forces may be operating and whatever the ethical level of staff behavior, the student actor in the situation learns some relevant lessons.

Case 5. On the first anniversary of the suicide of a student who leaped from the ninth story of a high-rise residence hall, a group of students dangles a dummy from an upper floor of the same hall and then allows it to fall to a roof below after it has attracted the attention of other students. Medical rescue personnel who are called to scene discover the "prank." The hall director and the dean of students are so incensed by the students' callous behavior that they resolve to identify and punish those responsible before the evening is over. Students residing on the floor from which the dummy was dropped are called in and interviewed one by one. While no direct accusations are made, it becomes clear that three students are likely to be the culprits. The three are called in individually. Each is told that he or she has been reliably identified, and each is given an opportunity to confess, leave the hall the next day, and be placed on probation. The students are also advised that the alternative to a confession is a Judicial Office hearing with expulsion from the university as the probable result. They confess. The dean and hall director are fully aware that there is insufficient evidence for a judicial hearing.

Case 6. Mary is a member of the counseling staff in a community college. As a part of her responsibilities, Mary teaches a group counseling course to fifteen students who are enrolled for credit. One day after class, Susie, a student in the group counseling course, comes and asks to talk privately with Mary. After an hour-long conference, Mary determines that Susie is a very disturbed young woman who needs intensive psychotherapy. The possibility is discussed with Susie, who agrees to seek therapy, but she wants Mary's advice on the selection of a therapist. Mary has been conducting her own private practice with the knowledge and approval of her supervisor. As the conversation continues, Susie expresses her high level of trust in Mary and asks if it would be possible for her to become one of Mary's private clients.

Case 7. The fraternity coordinator has learned that a "little sister" of one of the fraternities has filed rape charges against five members of the chapter. An investigation by the town police reveals that all five men acknowledge having had sexual relations with the young woman during the evening in question, but they also allege that she was a willing, if intoxicated, participant.

The district attorney concludes that there is no criminal case, and the "little sister" drops the charges. Since the fraternity house in question is not physically on the campus, and there is a college policy of referring "off-campus" matters to local authorities, there is little chance of pursuing the matter through the campus student conduct office.

Working with Student Organizations

Staff interactions with student organizations occur in relatively public, "for-the-record" circumstances that expose the ethical components of conflicts and decisions to scrutiny. Those circumstances carry some risk, for several reasons. Where professional staff consistently avoid the ethical components of decisions, students will be quick to perceive the pattern for what it is and conclude that morality and ethics are secondary to other, more practical issues. Even where attention to ethical issues is consistent and thoughtful, the complex task of sorting out conflicting principles may be beyond the comprehension of less thoughtful students, and principled staff members can wind up bearing the brunt of public criticism for principled action.

Case 8. A college student newspaper has won a series of prizes from journalistic societies for its tradition of agressive investigative reporting. The student editorial staff hears a campus rumor that sedatives, sleeping pills, and tranquilizers are freely dispensed by the physicians and nurse practitioners at the student health service. Three reporters are coached on the symptoms related to sleep disturbances and depression and present themselves to the health service for treatment. Each student receives medications that are available only by prescription. Based on this investigative reporting, the paper prints a two-part series alleging the careless dispensing of prescription drugs. The student affairs vice-president requests information from the health service about the matter and learns that two of the three students were referred to the mental health unit for follow-up; the students could not receive additional medication until the referral was completed. Moreover, the physician director also provides information showing a drug-dispensing pattern that is substantially more conservative than prevailing community standards in the private practice of medicine. Some modest detective work yields the names of two of the reporters, and the vice-president refers them to the campus conduct officer for "providing false information to a university official" — a violation of the student conduct code. The paper takes its case to the regional press, which in turn accuses the vice-president and the college of actions that exert a chilling effect on First Amendment rights.

Case 9. Sally is the director of a 500-bed residence hall. Not long ago, she began to date Jack, an undergraduate resident in her hall. Jack and Sally spend much of their free time together. Jack has made it very obvious both to a number of other residents of the hall and to hall paraprofessional staff that he has moved into Sally's apartment.

Case 10. The student union program board is planning its annual "filthy flick festival," and the center director reminds board members of the protest made by the board of trustees the year before. The director also points out that several state legislators have threatened restrictive legislation that would serve to censor films at state-sponsored institutions; the legislation may be unconstitutional. The student board members reply that student fee monies support their programming and that the event is popular with students. They also suggest that the legislature should be confronted if unconstitutional laws are proposed or enacted. The union director is really more concerned about the sexually demeaning content of the proposed films but feels compelled to consider the issues of censorship and of maintaining an open forum on campus.

Case 11. Doctor Y, a psychologist on the staff of the college counseling center, has established strong and effective ties with members of the campus gay/lesbian community and has acted as a reconciling force when conflicts have arisen between gays and other campus and community groups. With the consent of the counseling center's director, Doctor Y offers a sexual enrichment workshop for gays and lesbians. The dean of students complains to the center director when advertisements for the workshop appear in the campus newspaper; there have been a number of complaints from members of the college governing board and from not a few parents.

Interactions with Colleagues

Confronting a colleague with an actual or presumed ethical lapse may be the single most difficult task that a professional will face. To be confronted by a colleague and have one's ethical conduct questioned could be the most painful experience in a professional career. It probably makes very little difference whether the colleague is another student services professional, an administrative associate in another division, or a member of the faculty. Most individuals become defensive when faced with such charges, and the encounter becomes highly emotional. Even when there is an inclination to be reflective about the issue in question, variations in personal value systems, conflicting philosophical positions, and even allegiance to different professional ethical codes can make resolution difficult. The special responsibility to model ethical conduct for student constituents calls for a standard of behavior that probably does not exist in the private sector. And, the quality of faculty and staff ethical transactions sets the tone for student interactions.

Case 12. A university counseling center psychologist has a counseling relationship with Tammie, who lives in Brown Hall. John, the head resident in Brown Hall, calls the psychologist to discuss a matter in connection with her role as the assigned consultant for mental health issues in Brown. John reports that the entire hall is being disrupted by Tammie's suicide threats. The psychologist is quite certain that the threats are manipulative in character but does not have a signed release from Tammie to talk with John.

Case 13. A woman graduate student from the Middle East has been "pressured" into having sexual intercourse with her major adviser. She cannot tell her husband, because he would disown her. She cannot return to her own country, because she would be dishonored on two counts—the "adultery" and the failure to complete her degree. She reports the matter to the director of the campus women's center, who understands the need for privacy, the student's fear of consequences if the major adviser is confronted, and the student's need to have someone to talk to. The director also considers the adviser's behavior to be a form of sexual assault committed by a university employee.

Case 14. Jill and Sara are members of the senior staff in a large residence hall. Sara runs a number of human relations and communications skills workshops as a part of her contribution to educational programs in the residence halls. Jill has become concerned about the impact of some of the workshop exercises on a few participants, who leave the sessions either in tears or quite depressed.

Case 15. You completed interviews for a new and attractive position two weeks ago. The chair of the search committee calls to say that you are the committee's first choice and offers you a substantial increment over your current salary. You agree to accept the offer and tell the chair that you will confirm by mail very shortly. In the meantime, you tell your boss about your decision. Your boss comes back a few hours later with a counter offer authorized by the college president that is better than the offer you just received from the other college.

Case 16. Over after-work cocktails, the dean of students is unburdening to two colleagues, the college business manager and the academic dean. The problem at hand is the absence of moving expenses for a cherished candidate for placement director. The state simply provides no money for moving expenses, and there are no other sources of funds for this purpose. The academic dean suggests putting the director on salary for three weeks before she assumes her assigned duties, thus generating the needed money. The candidate appears to have an equal offer at a sister institution. The college business manager supports the academic dean's suggestion, indicating that this is how the college has handled the matter for years.

Supervisory Relationships

The power accorded to those in supervisory positions also provides opportunities for abuse. Accordingly, movement up the administrative ladder is probably accompanied by proportionally increasing responsibility to be aware of the ethical consequences of personnel decisions. Despite the substantial value that higher education communities place on collegiality in the work setting, subordinate staff tend to perceive the distance between themselves and supervisors as greater than the supervisors do. Differences in perceptions can cause a supervisor to underestimate the extent to which subordinates are vulnerable and deferential to subtle cues or the difficulty that staff may have in confronting a supervisor with behaviors that they find objectionable. It should also be noted that subordinate staff owe supervisors certain loyalties and ethical commitments. Middle managers and senior administrators invest a substantial amount of energy in staff welfare. A rapid leap to the conclusion that one's boss is ill intentioned has its own ethical implications.

Case 17. A member of your staff has developed very strong human relations training skills and conducts a relatively small consulting business with various organizations in the region. On some of the days that your staff member is absent from the office, she tells you that she has consulting work and is taking vacation days. You suspect, however, that some of her sick days are also consulting days and that she is trying to save as many vacation days as possible. She rarely fails to complete her assigned work for your office, although she appears harried and overworked on occasion.

Case 18. The assistant director of your career planning and placement office has just completed coordinating and implementing the conversion of your records and credentials system to a computerized entry and retrieval operation—a year-long task involving innumerable hassles with other college entities. The assistant director brought it all off with skill and patience. During the last four months of the process, the assistant director was also involved in difficult marital problems, which culminated in a separation. This staff member is clearly fatigued and in need of a break. You are aware of a national conference in a pleasant resort area that has marginal value to the assistant director and your office, and you offer to pay the travel expenses and registration fee, urging the staff member to add a couple of vacation days to both ends of the conference. The resulting cost exceeds the assistant director's annual travel allowance, but you press the staff member to accept.

Case 19. The chair of the staff development committee arranges for a showing of the film, "Pink Triangle," which traces the history of oppression and discrimination against gays and lesbians over the past fifty years. The directors of housing and of student activities recommend the film to their staffs for use with student groups in residence halls and campus student organizations. A number of activities coordinators and hall directors find the film personally objectionable and state their unwillingness to show a film to students that "promotes immoral behavior."

Case 20. As dean of students, you are holding your annual opening session with your professional staff, a gathering of some thirty people. During a question-and-answer period toward the end of the meeting, one staff member challenges you on a particularly sticky new college policy affecting staff vacations. The policy was introduced last spring, you had opposed it in private meetings with your president, and the staff is generally aware that you had done so. You cut off the offender with flippant, sarcastic response, and the meeting closes with no further questions from staff. As you leave the meeting, it occurs to you that you may owe the staff member an apology. At the same time, you are reluctant to give him any satisfaction, since he consistently presses the limits on any policy matter and acts out the role of rebel in virtually all staff meetings. You also wonder where the apology should be made, if it is to be made at all. If the offense was given in public, should not the apology also be made in public?

Case 21. George has established a reputation as an innovator in placement and has built his campus agency into a model of what a developmentally focused agency can accomplish with both students and prospective employers. Before George assumed the director's position, the placement office was quite traditional in focus and only marginally effective. George has recruited a bright, creative, and energetic young professional staff over the past three years. A small nucleus of this group of career counselors has begun to challenge George on issues related to program focus, and its members are pressing hard for more time to pursue their particular interests. George has resisted some of their suggestions, because he judges that they could have the effect of scattering staff and fiscal resources and thus of undercutting programs that are currently very effective. Having lost the battle in staff meetings, the dissident group loses little time in proclaiming their discontent and dissatisfaction to peers at other institutions and in sharing their judgment that George is rigid and unresponsive to staff input.

Special Populations

Just what constitutes proper action in response to populations with perceived special needs has been and will continue to be a topic of debate in the academic community for some time to come. For that matter, there is little agreement about what groups need to be accorded protected status in matters of access to programs, jobs, and professional advancement. It has not been long since college and university presidents (along with more than a few student services professionals) were publicly bemoaning the "unreasonableness" of the federal requirement that every campus needed to modify its architecture and its services so as to accommodate the physically handicapped. Having experienced the enrichment that the visually, hearing-, and mobility-impaired have brought to our campuses, we now wonder at our initial resistance, let alone our insensitivity. The gaps between the public positions taken by institutions of higher education and the professional associations and daily practices on our campus with respect to oppressed classes of individuals remain a source of pain for many of our students and colleagues. Consistent examples of covertly expressed prejudice, persistent insensitivity, and near-blatant pursuit of self-interest combine to suggest that equity for all members of the academic community is an ethical ideal that requires exceedingly persistent attention.

Case 22. Sam works for a student services agency that has had women on the professional staff for only the last three years. There are now four women programmers on the staff, and it is Sam's private conclusion that the quality of agency work has improved as a consequence of their presence, drive, and professionalism. Jim, an agency colleague, is about two years shy of retirement and generally "walks" through his professional day carrying slightly less than his share of the agency work load. Jim has good contacts in sister agencies, and his judgments are well regarded by senior administrators. The agency has benefited financially and otherwise as a consequence of his clout. Jim's interactions with new women staff members are characterized by the giving of "friendly advice" (which the women find patronizing), by persistent references to them collectively as "the girls," and by the offering of "counsel" on how to get ahead in the agency and division that seems designed to intimidate and depress. Sam feels a need to confront Jim with the effects of his behaviors toward the women staff members but is not sure how to carry it out. Besides, he is doubtful that doing so is worth the effort, given the fact that Jim is only two years away from retirement.

Case 23. The affirmative action office of your college has persuaded the senior administration that the time has come to press for significant progress in the hiring of protected class individuals. They target all vacancies for members of these groups, although many on the staff and in federal enforcement agencies believe that such a practice is unfair, illegal, or both. All position announcements, as usual, carry the AA/EEO designation, but there is nothing to indicate the strong likelihood that preference will be given to protected class members over white males. The directive has come from the president's office; your immediate supervisor has a tendency to avoid making waves and to punish those who do. You agree with the general intent of the directive, for you believe that protected classes are genuinely underrepresented on campus. However, you are disturbed by what you believe to be misleading advertising that could cause no nonprotected groups to receive serious consideration for any of the positions. You have just agreed to chair a search committee.

Case 24. A search committee presents you with three candidates for an important mid-level management position. In ranked order, the first two appear to be very close in qualifications and ability and the other a distant third. The first-ranked is your choice by a slight margin. He has indicated to you in the course of your interview that he has a degenerative disease that could leave him totally incapacitated. Whether the disease would progress to that point in three, five, or ten years can only be a matter of conjecture. You share this information with your president and vice-president colleague as you prepare to make the hiring decision. The vice-president points to the financial obligations that the institution is likely to incur as a consequence of total disability and urges you to make the offer to the second-ranked candidate. The president seems inclined to agree, adding a comment to the effect that senior officers also have the responsibility of fiscal accountability to the governing board.

Governing Boards and External Constituencies

Both private and public institutions have publics and patrons who understand themselves as having legitimate interest and equity in matters of institutional goals, policies, and practices. Those equity holders include parents, taxpayers, donors, legislators, governing board members, employers of graduates, alumni, residents of the community in which the institution is located, and special-interest groups with a commitment to particular social or political values. The student services professional shares with other academic colleagues a responsibility to assert the values that sustain institutions of higher education and to assist these publics in understanding why those values must be maintained. Similarly, members of the academic community owe external constituencies the courtesy of careful listening and thoughtful consideration of expressed views and concerns. Our skills and comfort with words have too frequently led others to perceive academics as being arrogant in style and patronizing in intent.

Case 25. Jane, a student affairs specialist, organized a panel presentation for Women's Week activities. Jane asked her friend Sue, a local community activist, to participate in the panel. Sue was an active candidate for state representative and asked Jane for permission to use five or ten minutes of her presentation to talk about her candidacy and her positions on some important issues. Jane agreed but suggested that Sue wait until the end of the program to address those matters. In that way, she could integrate issues related to her candidacy into the question-and-answer part of the session. The day after the panel presentation, the vice-president called Jane into the office.

Case 26. Chris, director of placement, learns that two major accounting firms have canceled their interview schedules for the coming year. As a routine follow-up, she calls the personnel officers at the two firms and discovers that Les, chair of the college's accounting department, has established his own consulting and placement agency as a private venture and that the two firms in question are conducting their interviews of the college's students and alumni through his agency. When Chris calls Les to express her concern about potential conflicts of interest, Les points out that he charges the firms only a modest placement fee and that he views this portion of his agency's actaivities as a service to the graduates of his department.

Case 27. The president of a major state university consistently receives requests from legislators to find a place in the fully booked residence halls for one or more of their constituents. These requests commonly come within six weeks of the beginning of the fall term. A few of these legislators have been good friends of the university, helping to pass legislation critical to its fiscal and programmatic welfare. After a year in which the vice-president for student affairs has had to seek such places from housing staff (thus placing students with earlier application dates on a waiting list), he proposes an alternative to the president and to the director of housing. At the beginning of the application season, ten beds in residence halls will be set aside for assignment exclusively by the president's office. Any of the ten beds remaining unassigned by the last week before classes start will revert back to the housing office for assignment.

Some Next Steps

In this opening chapter, we have illustrated the complexity and diversity of professional behaviors that seem likely to have ethical implications. Obviously, we have not provided answers. To attempt to do so is to engage in an exercise in dualistic thinking and thus to defeat the purpose of this sourcebook.

The chapters that follow offer opportunities to use principles as aids in ethical problem solving, some matrices that enable us to define behaviors of high ethical quality, and critical reviews of established ethical codes affecting the student services professions. One way of reaching the goal of enhancing the general level of ethical conduct is to use the tools offered in the next three chapters to assess the cases just described.

References

Bok, D. *Beyond the Ivory Tower: Social Responsibilities of the Modern University.* Cambridge, Mass.: Harvard University Press, 1982.

Brubacher, J. S. *On the Philosophy of Higher Education.* (Rev. ed.) San Francisco: Jossey-Bass, 1982.

Harry J. Canon is professor of leadership and educational policy studies at Northern Illinois University and current chair of the Professional Ethics and Conduct Committee of the American College Personnel Association.

We must consider ethical principles and theories in order to make reasoned and ethically defensible judgments in student affairs.

Ethical Principles and Ethical Decisions in Student Affairs

Karen Strohm Kitchener

College student personnel work has ethical issues and ethical choices at its very core. The cases presented by Canon in Chapter One show how student affairs professionals daily make ethical choices that have serious consequences for students, other professionals, and themselves. This is true at an abstract level as well, since most student services professionals identify helping the individual and promoting the good of society as parts of their dual role. For example, the preamble of the ethics code of the American College Personnel Association (ACPA) (Appendix 1) advocates enhancing "the worth, dignity, potential, and uniqueness of each individual" and, as a consequence, serving society. Further, as Chickering (1981, p. 10) has argued, "Every college and university, public or private, church related or not, is in the business of shaping human lives. They will continue to be. It is one of the fundamental reasons for their existence." These goals—to benefit students and to shape their lives—are by their very nature ethical ones, since they involve making judgments of value about people and their lives (Taylor, 1978).

The model of ethical decision making presented in this chapter is designed to help practitioners understand and define the choices they face. It does not offer absolute answers. Rather it illustrates how professionals can make reasoned and ethically defensible judgments.

A Model of Ethical Decision Making

The model of ethical justification described in this section draws heavily on the work of Beauchamp and Childress (1979) and of Drane (1982). The works of these authors should be consulted for further discussions of the principles. The implications of the model for the helping professions have been elaborated by Kitchener (1984b).

The model proposes that ethical decision making is always a matter of a particular situation and that the facts of that situation dictate the ethical rules, ethical principles, and ethical theories that have relevance for a decision. It also suggests that the process of ethical justification is hierarchically tiered. There are three increasingly general and more abstract levels of ethical reasoning; appeals can be made to a higher level if a lower, more specific level fails to provide the rationale for a decision. According to the model, the first line of ethical defense consists of professional rules and codes of ethics. The next level, ethical principles, provides a general ethical framework for identifying the critical issues at stake and deciding among them. At the highest level, ethical theories provide a rationale for deciding when ethical principles are in conflict. For example, in case 5, three students are pressured to confess to an offense that they probably committed. Based on the ACPA statement of ethical and professional standards (1981), which will hereafter be referred to as the *ACPA ethical code,* there is little question that the dean and hall director have some ethical responsibility to intervene, since, according to the code, student's freedom of choice may be limited when their actions could result in significant damage to others. In this case, there is reason to believe that the students' actions could cause psychological harm to other students who knew the suicide victim. At the same time, the ACPA ethical code also requires student affairs staff members to confront students in a "professional" manner. The question is, What constitutes a "professional" manner in this case? Was truth telling required of the dean and hall director when a good end could have been served by omitting information? The ACPA ethical code is silent on this issue. In contrast, at the level of ethical principles, the principle of justice requires that equals be treated as equals. From this perspective, the three students, despite the callousness of their actions, have a right to due process, just as other students do. Further, the principle of autonomy suggests that respecting others includes providing them with sufficient information to make informed choices. In this case, the information omitted was probably critical to the students' decision to confess. In other words, both ethical principles give good reason for suggesting that the dean and hall director showed poor ethical judgment. If the principles conflicted or if someone challenged the conclusion, the next tier in the model, that is, ethical theory, could provide further guidance.

Ethical Rules

Ethical rules provide the first level of ethical justification. In a professional organization, such rules are usually codified into a set of ethical standards, which professionals implicitly agree to follow by virtue of their membership in the organization. Ethical codes function somewhat like a set of laws for the organization (Kitchener, 1984a), since they are rules of conduct that are formally recognized as binding and that are enforced by a controlling authority, that is, the professional organization.

Some ethical issues can be adjudicated by direct reference to the ethical code. Thus, case 9, in which a head resident appears to be having a sexual relationship with an undergraduate student in her residence hall, can be decided by reference to the ACPA ethical code, which suggests that sexual relationships between professionals and students for whom the professional has supervisory responsibility have high risk for potential harm and that they are unethical.

Some would like to believe that ethical responsibilities are fulfilled if the ethical code of the profession is followed faithfully. This cannot be so. Ethical codes sometimes have omissions, or they offer contradictory advice. Further, university administrators have conflicting constituencies, to whom their ethical obligations will often differ. As Fargo (1981, p. 64) noted, "No code, no set of aspirations, however closely followed or devoutly emulated, can address the fundamental internal conflicts of interest that emerge from our job descriptions." Our codes sometimes acknowledge these conflicts, but they can never totally resolve them. For example, the ACPA ethical code says that members have responsibilities both to the individual and to the institution that employs them. In addition, the conflicting or confusing advice that a single ethical code sometimes gives is complicated because professionals frequently belong to more than one professional organization (Drane, 1982). In Chapter Four, Winston and Dagley discuss how the codes of student services organizations can conflict one with another. An act that is considered ethical by one organization can be considered unethical by another.

Ethical Principles

Ethical principles are more general, abstract, and fundamental than ethical codes. As a result, they provide a more consistent vocabulary or framework within which particular cases or issues can be considered. They not only provide a level of justification when ethical codes are silent or ambiguous, but they also provide a rationale for what the codes themselves include. For example, if the members of an ethics committee were challenged to explain why they should respect an individual's right of self-determination, they might refer to the principle of autonomy.

Four principles elaborated here—respecting autonomy, doing no harm, benefiting others, and being just—are drawn from the work of Beauchamp and Childress on biomedical ethics. The fifth principle—being faithful—draws on but goes beyond their work. This section draws on cases from Chapter One to illustrate each principle. The five principles are both necessary to and implicit in the ethical practice of student services work.

Respecting Autonomy. The concept of autonomy has long been seen as critical for ethical choice (Abelson and Nielson, 1967). The concept of autonomy has been understood to have two aspects. First, it includes the right to act as a free agent. Individuals have the right to decide how they live their lives, as long as their actions do not interfere with the welfare of others. Second, it includes freedom of thought or choice. Even in the most restricted environment (for example, a concentration camp, where individuals have little freedom to act), they retain the freedom to choose how to respond to others' actions and what they believe to be true or ethical.

Autonomy thus has implications both for how people see themselves and for how they view and act toward others. For example, it means that individuals have the right to make decisions about their lives, to choose future paths, or to decide whom to marry. But, the principle of autonomy also carries a responsibility toward others, for, if an individual wishes to be respected as a free agent, that individual must show respect for the rights of others. This is true even if he or she believes that the other person is mistaken. To do otherwise is to acknowledge that others may interfere in our lives when they believe us to be mistaken. Autonomy does not imply license to do whatever an individual chooses, as perhaps the students in case 5 would want to claim, since it is always limited by the need to respect the rights of others.

Making choices and acting as a free agent are dependent on rational decision-making processes. It does not make sense to suggest that infants are capable of autonomous choices, because they do not have the mental capacity to understand the consequences of their actions. For these reasons, autonomy is tied to the concept of competence. An individual's choice may be ignored if there are good ethical reasons for doing so and if the individual is judged to be incompetent. Philosopher Ruth Macklin (1982, p. 337) notes that it would be as unacceptable ethically to interfere with others' lives and violate their freedom if they are competent as it would be to allow "harm, destruction, or even death to befall an innocent, helpless human who is unable to make a reasonable choice."

However, competence is difficult to determine, and there are no absolute criteria for dichotomizing incompetence and competence. People are usually neither totally incompetent nor totally competent in all situations. At the same time, several factors are relevant in evaluating competence, particularly in college students. These factors include age, mental status (for example, depression), alcoholism, or drug abuse. Powell (in press) presents a thorough discussion of competence.

Because most college students are legally accorded the status of adults and because there is evidence to indicate that they make no worse choices than other adults, their autonomy needs to be respected. However, because in most cases their lives are still before them, because their judgment may not be totally mature, because their competence may be limited by situations or emotional factors, staff have an ethical responsibility to assess competence carefully.

Powell (in press) suggests that, as the consequences of the decision become increasingly critical (for example, life-threatening), the criteria for assuming competence should decrease. Thus, the college student who consistently abuses alcohol may ethically be required to seek counseling against his or her will, both because the student's competence is limited by alcohol and because the situation may be life-threatening (for example, an overdose may lead to death).

The principle of autonomy is the basis for several ethical rules frequently found in the ethical codes of student affairs professionals. These rules include the right of self-determination, the right to privacy or confidentiality, and informed consent. The right to privacy and confidentiality follows from the assumption that autonomous people have the right to make free decisions about their own lives. Informed consent and the First Amendment right of free speech protect the individual's right to have full information when he or she is faced with making a decision about his or her life.

Several cases described in Chapter One involve issues of autonomy. Case 8 is particularly troublesome, because it involves the First Amendment right to free speech, the autonomous right of the reporters to write an article on the health center, and the right of the university community to have full and complete information about the health service. In this case, by providing inaccurate information, the student reporters infringed on the rights of the university community. They may also have unwittingly caused others harm by undermining confidence in the health service and by damaging the reputation of its staff. Clearly, their actions were unethical, especially if the inaccuracies were deliberate or the consequence of their failure to exercise due care. At the same time, freedom of the press has been jealously guarded in this country because of the belief that an informed electorate needs full information in order to make rational choices. Further, the university is recognized by government as an institution in which freedom of speech must be enhanced in order to protect the search for truth. Freedom of speech must be curtailed only when the ethical justification is overwhelming (Chambers, 1981). Thus, no matter what action is taken in this case, its aim should be to encourage the availability of full and accurate information. It is debatable whether the actions of the vice-president served this aim. Requesting a retraction, a more accurate disclosure of health center policies, and a public apology might have more fully protected the autonomy of all parties. Cases 2, 12, and 13 all involve the right of an autonomous person to decide who has information about his or her life.

Doing No Harm. Many ethicists (Beauchamp and Childress, 1979; Frankena, 1963; Ross, 1930) have suggested that doing no harm to others (also termed *nonmaleficence*) is a bsic ethical principle. All other things being equal, it is an even stronger ethical obligation than benefiting or helping others. The principle of above all doing no harm includes not engaging in activities that run a high risk of harming others.

Harm can be both physical and psychological. While physical harm leaves rather concrete traces, psychological harm is more difficult to define, and as a consequence it is more difficult to document. In fact, student services practitioners need to be particularly sensitive to subtle psychological harm, since university policies and actions may have long-term negative consequences on an individual's sense of self-worth and on his or her opportunities for advancement. One of the arguments for providing equal access to campus facilities for handicapped students and employees was that the failure to do so caused long-term psychological harm by denying a group of people potential for vocational advancement.

Case 14 involves a rather clear-cut issue of harm. In this case, it is Jill's ethical responsibility to bring the potential harmful effects of the human relations training to the attention of the group leader. It is the responsibility of both Jill and the group leader to try to determine whether the participants' tears reflect temporary discomfort associated with growth or the potential for long-term damage to self worth. Such a determination involves a judgment on the part of both women—a judgment that is difficult to make. At the same time, there is some empirical evidence (Bergin and Lambert, 1978) that human potential groups can be for better or for worse. As a general rule, the ethical obligation for intervention increases with the risk and magnitude of harm (Beauchamp and Childress, 1979). Several other cases described in Chapter One involve issues of harm. For example, Cases 21 and 22 involve subtle, unwitting psychological harm. Cases 4, 8, 10, and 13 illustrate conflicts between the potential for harm on one hand and issues of autonomy on the other.

Benefiting Others. Benefiting others (also referred to as *beneficence*) is an acknowledged goal of student services professionals. Student services exists to aid students in their intellectual, moral, and personal development. This goal is explicitly recognized in the ACPA mission statement that underscores the organization's commitment to fostering human development in higher education. Thus, acting ethically means not only preventing harm and respecting autonomy but actively promoting the health and well-being of others.

As Baumgarten (1982) noted, the concept of responsibility within professions can be traced back as far as Socrates, who claimed that no craft or profession should seek its own advantage but that it should instead benefit those who are subject to it. Further, Chambers (1981) has argued that institutions of higher education are charitable enterprises; many operate with state funding, and none are taxed. As a consequence, they have an obligation to benefit society. Thus, both because of professional commitment and because the profession operates within institutions dedicated to the service of society, student affairs professionals have an ethical obligation to benefit others.

The ethical responsibility to benefit others is not, however, without ethical dilemmas. Frequently, it is necessary to weigh doing no harm to a particular individual or group of individuals against benefiting others or the institution as a whole. Such is the issue in case 27, in which a university president must weigh a state legislator's request for a special favor to one student against the long-term good of the university community as it is affected by fair treatment of other students.

In cases where there is potential for harm as well as for benefit, many ethicists (Beauchamp and Childress, 1979; Abelson and Nielson, 1967; Ross, 1930) suggest that ethical responsibility lies in finding the greatest balance of value over disvalue. Called the *balancing principle,* it is derived from John Stuart Mill's utilitarian ethic. Most twentieth-century ethicists take this principle to mean that, when ethical principles conflict, the potential for good in all its ramifications must be balanced against the potential for harm (Kitchener, 1984a). In case 27, the balancing principle would require the university president to consider the possible consequences of refusing the state legislator's request. If refusing it would mean destroying the legislature's good will toward the university and thereby threatening the ability of the university to serve its students, the compromise worked out by the vice-president seems fair for all concerned. However, for the university president to deny the legislator's request because it was unfair to other students might benefit the university's reputation for being fair, do less harm to the students who applied on time, and encourage the legislator's constituents to be more responsible. While the second solution seems somewhat idealistic, perhaps part of the reason why universities have lost the favor of the communities in which they exist and why their reputation for offering moral leadership has diminished is because they fail to live up to their own ideals. Other cases in which benefiting others needs to be balanced against potential harm are 18, 19, and 20.

The other principle against which benefiting others often needs to be balanced is the principle of autonomy. Emphasizing help to others at the expense of their autonomy leads to paternalism. Paternalism presumes that the person in authority knows what is good for an individual and that the authority may undertake to regulate an individual's behavior against his or her will. Beauchamp and Childress (1979) suggest that such a strong paternalistic stance is seldom ethically justifiable. However, weak paternalism can in some cases be ethically justifiable when the person is not competent to make rational decisions and when serious harm would result from allowing the person to act freely.

Paternalism would not ethically justify breaking the confidence of the client in case 13. She appears competent to make her own decisions, she understands the implications of her choices, and she is not causing harm to others. The most ethical action for the director of the women's center to take may be to help the student devise other alternatives for working with the faculty member, for example, by acting as her advocate with him. Further, she may ask the student to reconsider her decision not to take action against the faculty member. However, it is not ethical to force others to press charges against someone, even when we believe them to be ethically obligated to do so. To take such action would be to violate the respect owed to another's autonomous choice. Issues involving a conflict between beneficence and autonomy are also involved in case 12.

Being Just. Justice in its broadest sense means fairness (Benn, 1967). Issues of justice commonly arise because of conflicts over limited goods and services. In other words, because goods and services are not always plentiful and because filling the needs of one group of individuals may mean reducing or limiting what another group receives, ways must be identified to distribute resources fairly. Clearly, such issues of distributive justice are critical in higher education today, since we are living in a time of limited and frequently declining budgets.

However, justice is broader than issues of distribution, since it also refers to fair treatment when the rights of one individual or group are balanced against another. In fact, Fargo (1981) argues that this sense of fairness is most critical to administration in higher education. Although it is not possible always to please all constituencies, it is important to assure that they receive fair representation when their interests clash.

Both senses of *justice* assume three standards: impartiality, equality, and reciprocity. Reciprocity is closely linked to what is known as the Golden Rule: Treat others as you would like to be treated yourself. Further, it means to give people the benefits that they are due. In higher education, the concepts of fair grade and fair salary carry this connotation. The assumptions of impartiality and equality can be traced to Aristotle's formal theory of justice, which suggests that equals should be treated equally and that unequals should be treated unequally if their differences are relevant to the case under consideration. This concept suggests, for example, that race, handicapping conditions, or sexual preference should not be considered in providing access to education, since none of these factors is relevant to the need for education. However, differences (that is, inequalities) in background may be relevant when considering the services that a group needs in order to make use of the educational environment. One group may need different (unequal) treatment (for example, special support services for educationally disadvantaged minorities, elevators for physically handicapped students) in order to make effective use of the university. Benn (1967, p. 299) reiterates this point by noting that justice does not mean that all people should be treated alike but that "the onus rests on whomever would treat them differently to distinguish them in relevant ways."

Helping to develop a rational, informed electorate that is committed to fair treatment for all is part of the obligation that the university owes to society. Learning does not take place through formal course work alone. It also involves the modeling and actions of university representatives. At a more abstract level, Rawls (1971) argued that all reasonable people need to be committed to justice because they are engaged with others in joint ventures which require them to cooperate in order to promote their common interests. If individuals expect others to be fair to them and to respect their interests, they must treat others fairly in return.

Two cases, 5 and 8, discussed earlier in this chapter involve issues of justice. In addition to the principles already reviewed, deciding whether the treatment of the students in these cases was ethical requires asking the question, Were they treated the same way as other students who had broken the same university rule, and, if they were not, were the differences of such a nature or extent as to require unequal treatment? In case 5, the students did not receive the judicial hearing that the university required in similar cases. Despite the fact that their action showed extremely poor taste, their callousness was not relevant to waiving the requirements of justice. If this standard prevailed in society at large, authorities would have the right to deny a trial to anyone whose actions offended them. In case 8, the question is, Does describing false symptoms to a health service constitute providing false information to a university official? If it does, then referring the student reporters to the university conduct officer was probably justified. If it does not, then the action taken by the vice-president may have been wrong, since it violates the notion that equals should be treated equally.

When dealing with issues of justice, it is important to remember that guaranteeing equal treatment, equal access to facilities, or due process for all does not always guarantee an equal outcome for everyone, nor does it ensure an outcome that seems intuitively to be fair. It is never possible to guarantee what will happen in the future, since too many variables are outside our control. On the other hand, acting justly increases the probability that the outcome will be fair. This is a fundamental assumption in a society ruled by law. Thus, in case 5 it may be that, if the authorities act fairly, the perpetrators of the offense may not be punished. However, the consequences of abandoning fair treatment are, in the long run, much worse. Other cases involving issues of justice are 1, 3, 10, 20, 22, 23, and 24.

Being Faithful. Ramsey (1970) argued that faithfulness or fidelity is central to all professions that are involved in helping others, since it involves issues of loyalty, truthfulness, promise keeping, and respect. Beauchamp and Childress (1979) suggest that the obligation to be faithful derives from the respect due to autonomous people. Lying, misinformation, and deceit all deny access to information that individuals need in order to make a free choice about participating in a relationship. Similarly, failing to live up to a pledge or agreement (for example, to respect confidentiality) disregards the person's choice to enter into a relationship that has certain expectations and limits. Ramsey (1970) argued, however, that fidelity is a separate ethical principle, which is at the core of the relationship between people. If people were not faithful to each other, no meaningful human bonds could exist.

Even if all people are not bound by the principle of being faithful, those in the helping professions acquire a special obligation to be so by virtue of the roles ascribed to them: that is, to help, to be deemed trustworthy. This special ethical obligation can be thought of as an implicit contract or agreement between professionals and those with whom they work not to exploit, lie to, or otherwise deceive those in their professional care. Without such a contract, student services would be ineffective.

Chambers (1981, p. 6) defines *contract* as "an agreement between parties that each will fulfill certain obligations or honor certain duties in return for privileges or benefits offered by the other"; he holds that the concept of contract is central to the university's obligations toward its constituents. For example, by accepting students, the institution agrees to be faithful in educating them. Students also incur certain ethical obligations, for example, to abide by the rules of the institution (Kitchener, 1984b).

As Chambers (1981) points out, the fairness of ethical contracts in higher education is strongly influenced by the maturity and power of the parties involved, since a contract implies equality of strength and reason. It must be assumed that professionals and students are unequal in both regards; therefore, the contract or bond between staff and students is unequal. The inequality implies that the more powerful group has a greater ethical obligation. "To meet this ethical obligation, an institution must not just be fair and accurate but must add an extra measure of disclosure and explanation to ensure that students can intelligently consent to the contract" (Chambers, 1981, p. 8). This is especially true in institutions of higher education, because students are exposed to an environment in which the ambiguity and subjectivity of both knowledge and morality are deliberately explored. Developmentally, the potential for university staff to be influential for better or for worse in this process is well documented. As a consequence, the ethical responsibility to make the process is a positive one is enormous. Chambers suggests that, if the more sophisticated member of a contract creates deliberate misunderstandings either intentionally or by omission, the deception is an unconscionable breach of integrity; it may even relieve the less powerful person from complying with his or her part of the bargain.

Most of the cases described in Chapter One have implications derived from the expected bond between people. Case 1 is interesting because it involves an implicit contract between a faculty member and a student. On the one hand, the faculty member has the obligation to be fair, to be truthful, and to educate the student. On the other hand, the student has the responsibility to complete the required work. In this case, the student has fulfilled his part of the ethical contract. The faculty member, by contrast, may have failed to fulfill part of his ethical obligations. Educating graduate students includes educating them into the mores of the profession, including the rights and responsibilities surrounding publication. As a consequence, at a minimum the professor had a responsibility to inform the student before the project began about authorship of publications so the student could decide whether to proceed with the project under such conditions. At the same time, because of the potential in unequal relationships to misuse authority, faculty have a special obligation to be fair. It follows that, in cases where ownership of publications is not totally clear, faculty should err ethically on the side of the less powerful person. Following this line of reasoning, we may judge that the faculty member showed poor ethical judgment by failing to offer the student coauthorship. Other cases for which the principle of fidelity is relevant include those involving faculty and students (3, 13), staff members (5, 6, 9), and an employee and employer (11).

Ethical Principles: Absolute, Subjective, or an Alternative

Several authors (Baumgarten, 1982; Churchill, 1982; Kitchener, 1984b; Losito, 1980) have noted that professionals frequently believe they are caught on the horns of an absolutism-subjectivism dilemma when they think about ethical principles. Most contemporary moral philosophers (Abelson and Nielson, 1967) as well as most professionals writing in the area of applied ethics would agree that following moral principles absolutely would in some cases lead to immoral acts. For example, if truth telling were considered absolute, it could lead to the death of an innocent person if information was requested on the whereabouts of a Jew in Nazi Germany. Further, absolutism would be untenable in a university that values free and open inquiry. In addition, as it has already been noted, ethical principles sometimes conflict with each other and give contradictory advice about what is ethical.

At the same time, subjectivism—the claim that values are a strictly personal affair and that they have no greater validity—is equally untenable. For one thing, it leads to the position that everybody's moral behavior and judgment are equally valid. Such a claim does not make much sense when we compare, for example, Martin Luther King with Hitler. For another, subjectivism precludes judging an act as ethical or unethical by any group or set of ethical rules.

There is an alternative to absolutism or subjectivism, which many contemporary philosophers and practitioners endorse. Ethical principles may be considered as prima facie binding. The meaning of the term *prima facie* comes from law, where it means that something—for example, a principle—establishes an obligation unless there are circumstances or other obligations that are stronger. In this case, it means that ethical principles are more than convenient guidelines but less than absolutes. They are always ethically relevant, and they can be overturned only by stronger ethical obligations. In the case of telling a lie to save a life in Nazi Germany, truth telling remains ethically important, but saving a life is more important. In some ways, principles should be considered to be "conditional duties" (Abelson and Nielson, 1967). The conditions under which they may be overturned must always be ethically relevant.

Considering moral principles as prima facie valid leads to the view that sound ethical practice involves carefully reasoned judgments that weigh and evaluate the implications of the relevant principles for each case at hand. This position fits with the arguments of Baumgarten (1982), Churchill (1982), and Losito (1980), who all consider rational inquiry or reasoned arguments to be the basis for ethical decision making in applied professions. As Losito (1980,

p. 45) suggests, moral evaluation should be "conceived as a rational enterprise in which reasonable justification can be offered for the standards of human conduct."

Viewing ethical principles as prima facie valid does not relieve professionals from the burden of decision making in ethical cases. Instead, it plants the responsibility firmly on their shoulders, where justifiably it should lie, since professionals must ultimately answer for the consequences of their own decisions. However, while the principles do not provide absolute answers, neither do they lead to nihilism, for they provide consistent, cross-situational advice on which ethical actions and decisions can be based.

Further, as the model introduced at the opening of this chapter suggests, when ethical principles give conflicting advice it may be necessary to move to the highest level of ethical reasoning, that of ethical theory, for help in resolving the differences. While a discussion of ethical theories is beyond the scope of this chapter, it should be noted that many twentieth-century ethicists (Abelson and Nielson, 1967; Baier, 1958; Toulmin, 1950) suggest that all ethical decisions should be universalizable or generalizable. This means that, when we must decide between moral principles, we should decide in a way that is consistent with what we would want for ourselves, our loved ones, and all others under the same circumstances. In addition, we should decide in a way that would lead to the least amount of avoidable harm.

References

Abelson, R., and Nielson, K. "History of Ethics." In P. Edwards (Ed.), *The Encyclopedia of Philosophy. Vol. 3.* New York: Macmillan, 1967.

American College Personnel Association. "Statement of Ethical and Professional Standards." *Journal of College Student Personnel,* 1981, *42,* 184-189.

Baier, K. *The Moral Point of View.* Ithaca, N. Y.: Cornell University Press, 1958.

Baumgarten, E. "Ethics in Adademic Profession: A Socratic View." *Journal of Higher Education,* 1982, *53,* 282-295.

Beauchamp, T. L., and Childress, J. F. *Principles of Biomedical Ethics.* Oxford, England: Oxford University Press, 1979.

Benn, S. I. "Justice." In P. Edwards (Ed.), *The Encyclopedia of Philosophy. Vol. 4.* New York: Macmillan, 1967.

Bergin, A. E., and Lambert, M. J. "The Evaluation of Therapeutic Outcomes." In S. L. Garfield and A. E. Bergin (Eds.), *Handbook of Psychotherapy and Behavior Change.* New York: Wiley, 1978.

Chambers, C. M. "Foundations of Ethical Responsibility in Higher Education." In R. H. Stein and M. C. Baca (Eds.), *Professional Ethics in University Administration.* New Directions in Higher Education, no. 33. San Francisco: Jossey-Bass, 1981.

Chickering, A. W. "Introduction." In A. W. Chickering (Ed.), *The Modern American College: Responding to the New Realities of Diverse Students and a Changing Society.* San Francisco: Jossey-Bass, 1981.

Churchill, L. "The Teaching of Ethics and Moral Values in Teaching." *Journal of Higher Education,* 1982, *53,* 296-306.

Drane, J. F. "Ethics and Psychotherapy: A Philosophical Perspective." In M. Rosenbaum (Ed.), *Ethics and Values in Psychotherapy.* New York: Free Press, 1982.

Fargo, J. M. "Academic Chivalry and Professional Responsibility." In R. H. Stein and M. C. Baca (Eds.), *Professional Ethics in University Administration.* New Directions in Higher Education, no. 33. San Francisco: Jossey-Bass, 1981.

Fischer, K. W. "A Theory of Cognitive Development: The Control and Construction of Hierarchies of Skills." *Psychological Review,* 1980, *87,* 477-531.

Frankena, W. K. *Ethics.* Englewood Cliffs, N. J.: Prentice-Hall, 1963.

Kitchener, K. S. "Ethics in Counseling Psychology: Distinction and Directions." *Counseling Psychologist,* 1984a, *12,* in press.

Kitchener, K. S. "Intuition, Critical Evaluation, and Ethical Principle: The Foundation for Ethical Decisions in Counseling Psychology." *Counseling Psychologist,* 1984b, *12,* in press.

Kitchener, K. S. "The Reflective Judgment Model: Characteristics, Evidence, and Measurement." In R. A. Mines and K. S. Kitchener (Eds.), *Young Adult Cognitive Development: Characteristics, Environmental Influences, and Research Problems.* New York: Praeger, in press.

Losito, W. F. "The Argument for Including Moral Philosophy in the Education of Counselors." *Counseling and Values,* 1980, *25,* 40-46.

Macklin, R. "Refusal of Psychiatric Treatment: Autonomy, Competence, and Paternalism." In R. B. Edwards (Ed.), *Psychiatry and Ethics.* Buffalo, N. Y.: Prometheus, 1982.

Powell, C. J. "Ethical Principles and Issues of Competence in Counseling Adolescents." *Counseling Psychologist,* in press.

Ramsey, P. *The Patient as Person.* New Haven, Conn.: Yale University Press, 1970.

Rawls, J. *A Theory of Justice.* Cambridge, Mass.: Harvard University Press, 1971.

Rest, J. "Moral Development in Young Adults." In R. A. Mines and K. S. Kitchener (Eds.), *Young Adult Cognitive Development: Characteristics, Environmental Influences, and Research Problems.* New York: Praeger, in press.

Ross, W. D. *The Right and the Good.* Oxford, England: Clarendon Press, 1930.

Taylor, P. W. *Problems of Moral Philosophy.* Belmont, Calif.: Wadsworth, 1978.

Toulmin, S. *An Examination of Place and Reason in Ethics.* Cambridge, England: Cambridge University Press, 1950.

Karen Strohm Kitchener is an associate professor and training director of the Counseling Psychology Program at the University of Denver. She is active in the American College Personnel Association, and she has served two terms on the Executive Council of that organization.

A schema for examining the application of ethical principles provides a means for examining ethical obligations and resolving some ethical dilemmas.

A New Model for Defining Ethical Behavior

LuAnn Krager

In the preceding chapter, Kitchener presented five principles that can help to guide the student affairs professional through the process of making ethical decisions. This chapter describes a framework that allows these principles to be related to a series of professional work roles. The framework provides an opportunity for the professional to view ethical conflicts in student affairs practice, to suggest specific behaviors as ethical goals, and to analyze the quality of his or her own ethical behavior. This chapter reviews Kitchener's five ethical principles, describes the schematic framework, discusses how the framework can be used to identify ethical conflicts, and shows how it can be used to construct specific behavioral descriptions of ethical conduct.

The Principles

In Chapter Two, Kitchener offers five principles for ethical action: respect autonomy, do no harm, benefit others, be just, and be faithful. Respecting autonomy refers to freedom of action and freedom of choice. It includes the right to be autonomous and the responsibility to treat others as autonomous individuals. Doing no harm addresses the requirement of avoiding actions that harm others or that place them at risk. Benefiting others asks that professionals contribute to others' welfare and promote their growth. Being just calls for equal treatment and for avoidance of special consideration of irrelevant factors, such as race, sex, or socioeconomic status. Being faithful requires the keeping of promises and being loyal.

There may be ethical neglect if any of these five principles is not met. If the principles conflict, the dilemmas that arise can be complex and difficult to resolve. Suppose, for example, that a staff member gains information that his or her supervisor needs to know in order to make a responsible decision. The information, which has been shared by a colleague, was supposed to be confidential. Does the staff member break the promise (be faithful) in order to do good for another (benefit others)? Should a promise (be faithful to a colleague) be broken on behalf of loyalty (be faithful to a supervisor)?

The task of attempting to resolve conflicts among competing ethical principles becomes more manageable if ethical principles and professional duties are examined in a systematic manner. One means for doing so takes the form of a matrix that shows professional roles on one dimension and Kitchener's five ethical principles on the other. Specific behavioral expectations occur at the intersections of the dimensions. This chapter uses a matrix format to apply the ethical principles to student services practitioners. Brown and Krager (in press) used a similar matrix framework to explore the application of ethical principles to graduate faculty work roles and student responsibilities. Two different models of practice are used for this discussion: the student affairs administrator (Ambler, 1980), and the student development educator (Brown, (1980). Five roles were chosen for each model to represent major job responsibilities. The administrator model includes planner, resource manager, organizer/coordinator, staff development facilitator, and evaluator. Table 1 presents a matrix with the ethical principles of Chapter Two as one dimension and the administrator roles as the other dimension. Table 2 provides another such matrix for the student development educator roles of adviser, instructor, program planner, researcher, and mentor. The examples of behaviors in the tables are intended to be illustrative rather than comprehensive. By looking at selected categories and illustrations and discussing them, the applicability and the usefulness of the schema for considering the ethical responsibilities of student services professionals becomes apparent. A discussion of one row (the planner role across the five ethical principles) and of one column (the autonomy principle across five administrator roles) illustrates how the matrix might be used to describe possible behavioral implications for administrators.

Planner Role and Ethical Principles

Respecting Autonomy. Planning includes setting policies, standards, priorities, goals, and objectives. It is required of all student affairs administrators, and, depending on its purpose, it can vary widely in scope. A residence hall director may change policy by expanding front desk hours or student assistant duties. A change in institutional policy can increase tuition or reduce

Table 1. Ethical Principles and Administrator's Roles

Administrator	Respecting Autonomy	Doing No Harm	Benefiting Others	Being Just	Being Faithful
Planner Policies Standards Priorities Goals, objectives	Recognize individual rights and need for exception. Support other's right to question policy and act to change it. Accept personal responsibility to speak out for developmental priorities.	Assess and consult for informed decision making. Plan for long-range as well as present student, staff, and institutional development Avoid misinterpretation, withholding of information, and planning for personal goals and gain.	Coordinate planning with other areas and groups for shared purpose and mutual benefit. Incorporate knowledge of developmental theory for optimal growth and responsive intervention.	Acknowledge and encourage contribution from faculty, other divisions, professionals, and student groups. Accept and appreciate diversity; be open to new approaches and responsive to unique needs. Plan for the acceptance and enhancement of differences.	Honor agreements made to groups and individuals. Work to evolve espoused ideals into workable plans and policies. Adhere to policy and standards, or act responsibly and appropriately for change.
Resource Manager Facilities Equipment Materials Financing Time	Allow staff to express differing opinions. Permit staff discretion in managing resources in their charge (facilities, time). Support other's right to question use of resources (materials, finance). Accept responsibility to express priorities in allocation.	Monitor resources and consult for informed decision making. Do not let funding become the sole determinant of objectives. Avoid letting power group pressure dictate resource allocation. Avoid overloading staff; discontinue programs where appropriate.	Communicate to staff on resource availability and limits. Work toward application and acquisition of outside funding; keep institution informed for cooperative functioning. Be responsive to divisional and student needs. Search for creative directions that accomplish goals with limited expense.	Adopt budgeting system where equitable allocation, incorporating priorities where needed based on institutional objectives. Incorporate objective evaluation to help identify resource priorities. Be fair and reasonable in demands on resources as well as in allocating them.	Work to ensure that resource allocation is guided by institutional mission, goals, and objectives. Honor position's commitment to student and staff as well as to institution. Honor agreements made with groups and individuals. Support espoused ideals and plans with adequate resources.

Table 1. Ethical Principles and Administrator's Roles *(continued)*

Administrator	Respecting Autonomy	Doing No Harm	Benefiting Others	Being Just	Being Faithful
Organizer/ Coordinator	Allow staff freedom to express opinions.	Avoid hidden agendas and empire building.	Facilitate the interaction of talent, ideas, and information.	Offer comparable and reasonable communication to staff.	Honor position's commitment to students and staff as well as to institution.
Structure	Permit staff discretion in managing their activities.	Avoid tradition as the sole reason for keeping things, policies, and people where they are.	Provide clear and consistent delegation and assignment.	Be fair in demands on time, assignments of duties, and performance expectations.	Be consistent with institutional purposes, goals, philosophies, traditions, values, and style.
Communication	Encourage individual style and creativity in job performance.	Do not use subversive techniques to undermine a person, group, or proposal.	Work for open, effective communication.	Be open to contributions from staff, students, faculty, and alumni.	Accept final responsibility and accountability.
	Allow function areas to develop sense of group direction and purpose.	Do not manipulate decisions for personal power or gain.	Encourage collegial interaction and shared decision making.	Maintain fair and equal treatment to all constituent groups.	Work to maintain personal and professional perspective and commitment in self and others.
	Encourage staff authority and responsibility over projects.		Be supportive of other areas and their endeavors.	Recognize and reward achievements appropriately and comparably.	
			Initiate allied service and cooperative projects.		

Staff Development Facilitator	Permit staff flexibility in negotiating, designing, and selecting duties and activities.	Avoid "rewarding" the energetic staff member with inappropriately more to do.	Encourage staff to develop own projects and accept new responsibilities for growth.	Be available equally to staff for information and guidance.	Be supportive in times of performance error, misintention, and misunderstanding as well as accomplishment. Work to develop beyond it.
Staff selection, assignment, and growth	Allow expression of differing opinions, philosophies, and approaches.	Do not try to keep a staff member in a position for the good of the position and the neglect of the person.	Use each position as training for branching into other positions or moving to a level of increased responsibility.	Be fair in selection, assignments, praise, opportunities, and support.	Honor verbal agreements of opportunities and advancement.
	Encourage use of individual style and expertise in job performance.	Do not place a person in a job or project without needed training and/or guidance.	Develop and direct staff to new possibilities for development.	Encourage and consider contributions from all staff.	Support staff in the job search, contract negotiation, and divisional representation.
	Accept personal responsibility for leadership and staff development.	Avoid holding staff immobile by restricting experiences.	Enhance individual expertise and incorporate training and modeling.		
Evaluator	Specify and involve all audiences served by evaluation.	Avoid uninformed conclusions and personal bias.	Ensure that evaluation allows for discovery of new questions as evaluation develops.	Select impartial and qualified evaluation personnel.	Ensure that findings are used honorably.
Program and personnel Judgments of worth	Allow expression of differing opinions.	Do not limit evaluation to identifying weaknesses, program termination and staff dismissal.	Use assessment to be responsive to needs, and channel efforts to worthy endeavors.	Be open to data and contributions from all involved.	Honor agreement to incorporate and act on evaluation information.
	Encourage staff input on evaluation purpose, planning, and implementation.	Do not reduce problem under study to a false simplicity.	Incorporate formative evaluation to modify programs and personnel performance for optimal chance of success and effectiveness.	Offer comparable and reasonable efforts and requirements.	Remain supportive of program and staff through formative modifications.
	Permit flexibility in evaluation approach and use of findings.			Ensure work will be evaluated and reported in a fair, objective manner.	Honor decisions to continue staff or program with appropriate financing, autonomy, and personal encouragement.
	Ensure procedures for review and negotiation.				

financial aid. The challenge to the administrator is that the decisions made in planning by relatively few people can affect great numbers of people.

Setting direction and rules of governance is a difficult process. There is the vocal majority to consider as well as expediency, cost, and the numerous stakeholder groups—faculty, alumni, public, media, board of directors, students. There are also the less vocal, the isolated individuals, and the populations with special needs. Is the role of the administrator to represent diverse populations, individual expectations, or simply the majority? The process used to make planning decisions is as related to autonomy as the content of the decisions themselves is. Some groups may represent themselves well and ask only to be heard, some groups may choose not to speak or feel that it is futile, and some groups may not have enough information or may be ill informed. Autonomy recognizes the right of individuals to represent themselves and to take part in the planning processes that affect them. But, providing autonomy does not mean thrusting complete freedom on those who are not ready or competent to assume it. An administrator may need to provide information and counsel or to act as representative of groups or individuals who are not prepared for that level of responsibility.

Doing No Harm. Few administrators cause injury by intent. More commonly, harm results from a lack of awareness or simply from not taking the time to think a situation through. Naïveté, misinterpretation, lack of information, and time pressures result in uninformed decisions and in thinking that is limited by the immediate situation. Every effort should be made to gather needed data, assess the situation carefully, and consult with colleagues and outside sources. Having established goals provides guidance for immediate decisions, and, where deadlines are not critical, time needs to be taken so that decision outcomes can be tested against long-range plans.

To avoid harm, attention must be given to even the briefest of interactions. How often are students rebuffed by the common response that that is the way something has always been? Are they being taught the importance of purpose or that it is futile to question bureaucracy? It is disheartening to consider the ways in which it is possible to cause harm. Fatigue leads to poor judgment. Budget cuts, staff reductions, and organizational survival generate a sense that inappropriate methods are justifiable as long as they produce the desired results. Planning can be used to reduce needless injury by anticipating critical decisions, supporting and monitoring communication, and weighing judgments against a set of ethical values.

Benefiting Others. The diversity of roles and responsibilities in student services creates a challenge in maintaining unity of purpose. This diversity can isolate divisions and diffuse overall organizational goals (Dutton and Rickard, 1980). Even the loyalty expected of an individual practitioner spans institutional levels and areas. A residence hall director participates in planning for his or her specific residence hall, for the complex in conjunction with other hall directors, for the housing office, for the student affairs division, and for the institution. Planning for the individual residence hall may take precedence due to the daily demands of operation and the personal accountability that the hall director feels. Units that do not identify overall goals tend to serve their own needs, and the potential for self-serving increases where organizational goals are unclear, overlap, or compete (Richman and Farmer, 1974). The question then arises, Is doing good limited to the administrator's own niche in the institution, or does it expand to include the whole institution and its effects? If student services practitioners work for the total institution, planning must be coordinated with other areas and groups for shared purpose and mutual benefit. Joint planning meetings can be held regularly, and allied services and cooperative projects can be initiated wherever possible.

Coordination alone does not accomplish institutional and professional goals if planning does not include all that we know about individual and organizational growth. Planning at every level and segment of the institution should incorporate knowledge of developmental theory for optimal growth and responsive intervention. A commitment to developmental philosophy provides a reliable and positive guide to institutional planning as well as the glue that binds smaller units to the whole.

Being Just. The principle of justice can help to remind the planner for whom he or she does the planning and to whom he or she is accountable. An institution consists of many constituent groups with special interests and unique needs. Is it fair to decide what is best for an organization without consulting its membership? At the same time, interest groups can apply pressure. Some exert noticeably more influence than others. For example, if several alumni push for a policy change and remind the administration of their substantial donations to the institution, how should their interests be balanced against the needs of other constituents?

Justice calls for fair and equal treatment. This implies that institutional members, including faculty, administrators, alumni, and students, should be encouraged to contribute to organizational decision making either as individuals or as special groups. The level of contribution should be determined only by factors related to the specific issue. The planner must be careful to exclude age, sex, race, religion, socioeconomic status, wealth, physical attractiveness, and personal friendships where they are not relevant to the problem. Differing opinions can be an impetus for creative solutions, and as such they should be welcome in the planning process.

Being Faithful. It takes time and trust to establish relationships that support effective communication and that help new ideas to evolve into workable plans. The investment of time and the nurturing of trusting relationships are essential to the accomplishment of organizational goals. Planning also demands the interaction of diverse groups and the tedious process of turning intangible concepts into concrete action. Trust requires following through on commitments.

The principle to be faithful suggests some additional avenues to build needed trust. The planner can begin with the honest, straightforward presentation of information, clarifying what is possible and what cannot be promised regardless of its desirability. Commitments should be honored, and actions should be based on espoused ideals.

Administrator Roles and Respect for Autonomy

The examples in the preceding section show how the administrator's planner role interacts with the five ethical principles. Specific behavioral expectations can be generated as planning functions are assessed against specific ethical principles. No doubt there are additional behaviors that have equal validity. This section examines another dimension of the matrix. The ethical principles of respecting autonomy has some important implications for each of the administrative roles of resource manager, organizer/coordinator, staff development facilitator, and evaluator.

Resource Manager. Personnel, facilities, materials, equipment, and time represent precious resources that collectively and individually make a difference in the institution's ability to accomplish its missions. The resource manager is faced with a balancing act when he or she considers the importance of supporting autonomy in the various groups that have a stake in how those resources are to be expended. Students have a legitimate interest in establishing budgets for the expenditure of student fees, but the institution also has an obligation to assure a continuing quality of campus life. In his or her role as steward, the resource manager may need to struggle with opportunities for students to assume responsibility and thus enhance their growth as autonomous beings. Similar conflicts will be encountered as the respective needs and contributions of the various student services agencies become apparent and as those agencies administer and expend their resources. An appropriate balance between agency autonomy and divisional welfare (as perceived by the senior resource manager) is not always easy to sustain.

Organizer/Coordinator. As an organizer/coordinator the administrator organizes the various segments and levels of the institution and takes action to coordinate their operations. The responsibilities of the role include monitoring the chain of command, the flow of communication, and the distribution of power and authority. Examples of this activity may be seen in a dean's direction over several student services divisions, in a divisional supervisor's management of office staff, or in a residence hall director's coordination of food service, maintenance, and student assistants. The administrator has ultimate responsibility. He or she is expected to provide unity of command, but he or she must also recognize the needs and goals of the people who work in the area and be responsive to them (Dutton and Rickard, 1980). The manner in which authority is exercised can directly affect staff development and productivity. How can the administrator provide the leadership expected and still promote staff self-direction?

Specific leadership strategies emphasizing autonomy can be used to stimulate staff to extend beyond their work niche and take responsibility as an integral part of the organization. Autonomy suggests that the administrator encourages staff expression of opinions and discretion in managing their activities. Work groups should be supported in developing their own sense of group purpose; individual style should be encouraged, and creativity should be rewarded. Autonomy is not unmitigated freedom or a do-what-you-will attitude: It involves the developmental process of delegating management responsibility.

Staff Development Facilitator. The facilitator role includes staff selection, duty assignment, and the provision of growth opportunities for staff members. Canon (1980) cites three common premises for staff development: remediating the skills of the marginally trained, enhancing accountability to the institution, and providing professional development as the ultimate exercise of professional responsibility. Careful selection, matching of abilities wiwth job requirements, adequate training programs, and personal encouragement can maximize performance to achieve the first two goals, but what guides the third premise of continued development? How should staff development facilitators fulfill their professional responsibility?

Autonomy is at the core of this developmental task. As in the other applications of this principle, it must be incorporated by design in order to be effective. The premise of professional development goes beyond directed training. It uses the challenge of new opportunity. Staff members should be given flexibility in negotiating, designing, and selecting new duties and activities. Expression of differing opinions and approaches to professional growth can be encouraged as well as individual style and innovation. Both the challenge and the freedom offered must be tempered by staff readiness. The ultimate goal is to help staff to extend their abilities sufficiently to move past present positions into new areas and levels of responsibility. For example, a staff member whose only work experience has been in financial aids may be encouraged to assist on a project of interest in another agency. A housing supervisor can work with a residence director to develop skills relating to the whole housing operation rather than to the individual residence hall. And, staff may be encouraged to do research in an interest area, to initiate a project, or to develop and teach a class or workshop.

Evaluator. For many, the evaluation process elicits mixed reactions. It is considered essential, but it is often thought to focus on finding what is wrong with a program or job performance, not on identifying what is right. There is tremendous value in identifying what is successful and what modifications can be made to be more effective.

Evaluation consists of initiating appropriate research assessment techniques, and it culminates in an objective judgment of worth. Experimental rigor and impartiality may imply that the evaluator must maintain a formal distance, but evaluation can be more responsive and useful if those being evaluated help to design and take an active part in it (Brown, 1979). What should

Table 2. Ethical Principles and Educator's Roles

Educator	Respecting Autonomy	Doing No Harm	Benefiting Others	Being Just	Being Faithful
Adviser Advising: • admissions • undecided	Permit students flexibility in selecting courses, duties, activities, and experiences.	Avoid undue rigor in expectations and demands.	Make use of student competence and information in program and personal development.	Be available equally to all students for information, time, and energy.	Honor agreements made for providing contacts, referrals, and additional information.
	Encourage expression and contribution from all student organization members.	Avoid provoking stress; be attentive to other pressures.	Use individual and organizational decision making as opportunity to teach process as well as to find particular solution.	Be fair and objective in appraisals of performance.	Respect confidential nature of personal sharing.
Organizations: • Greek • residence hall • student government • judicial activities • programming	Support development of group purpose and interactive decision making.	Provide adequate training for students assuming leadership and group roles.		Encourage openness and tolerance in all student organization members to individuality and diversity inside and outside the group.	Continue to watch for opportunities that might be of benefit to the individual or group.
		Avoid too little attention and guidance in organizational advising.	Challenge individual and group to consider new interests, activities, and enterprise.		Remain supportive through difficulties. If an open door is offered; honor it.
Instructor Teaching in: • classroom-credit noncredit • in-service programs	Permit choice in learning modality and appropriate flexibility in content emphasis and evaluation strategies.	Adequately cover essential content.	Assess changing needs and interests; design program to address them.	Conduct fair evaluations.	Be available beyond instruction for consultation time.
	Allow expression of differing opinions.	Distinguish between personal opinion and fact.	Provide students opportunity to seek application of content.	Be responsive to individual student needs and the needs of special groups.	Incorporate feedback to improve instruction.
	Encourage involvement in selecting program topics and role in presenting.	Assess entering skills and readiness for course and training content.	Acknowledge individuality; work to make content meaningful.	Allow time to address individual concerns.	

Program Planner Content and design of: • programs • activities • courses • in-service training	Design program/course with sufficient breadth to allow exploration of individual interests. Encourage staff and student input in planning programs and training. Offer a diversity of programs to promote sampling of interests and new involvements.	Avoid development of a competitive climate in courses and training. Ensure that program/curriculum permits acquisition of necessary skills and knowledge.	Design programs/curriculum that provide for assessment and responsiveness to student needs. Keep program and content current.	Work to make activities and programs known and available to all students. Support programs addressing special groups and cultural awareness. Have comparable and reasonable course and activity requirements.	Honor professional commitment to broad-range developmental program planning. Maintain credibility; fulfill promise of what has been offered. Be consistent with program requirements.
Researcher • discovery and use of new information • professional involvement • development of skills	Promote student and staff inquiry and collaboration. Permit choice of appropriate topics and methodology for student course work and staff projects.	Keep current on new research. Teach research process as well as using assistants as labor. Model ethical research techniques.	Provide opportunities for sharing of research ideas. Encourage students and staff to creatively consider application of new research. Support appropriate testing of new programs; share with professional audience.	Be fair in awarding recognition for contributions to research projects. Provide equal opportunity for student and staff involvement. Insist on accurate data, confidentiality, and respectable reporting.	Assist students and colleagues in developing projects of research. Follow through on agreement of collaboration and support. Honor offers of sharing results and giving feedback to research participants.

Table 2. Ethical Principles and Educator's Roles (continued)

Educator	Respecting Autonomy	Doing No Harm	Benefiting Others	Being Just	Being Faithful
Mentor • formal • informal • modeling professional/personal life	Model life-style and professional attitudes that demonstrate whole range of development, not just the professional person. Recognize significant influence on mentees' decision making. Model personal and professional sharing that distinguishes mentoring from traditional advising.	Avoid using students against each other or against colleagues. Do not get students involved in departmental/divisional squabbles. Avoid using staff and student loyalty to fight personal battles. Do not expect or demand allegiance on issues.	Attend orientation/training program in formal mentoring project. Acquire system for recording and evaluating mentee's development. Encourage mentee life-style toward total personal growth.	Be tolerant and open to students and staff. Be equally available to all mentees. Be fair and objective in evaluating student performance and development.	Act consistently with espoused values across time and situations. Honor time and commitment to mentee and mentoring program.

be the role of staff members when it is their work that is being judged?

Autonomy suggests that staff should be able to represent themselves in processes that affect them. This involves encouraging their input on evaluation purpose, planning, and implementation. Conflicts must be considered by the evaluator, and flexibility must be permitted in the use of findings. Procedures for review and negotiation can be incorporated to aid communication throughout.

Ethical Principles and the Educator's Role

We have seen how addressing the role responsibilities of a student services administrator in light of Kitchener's five ethical principles serves to sharpen ethical concerns and obligations. As there is movement from one role to another and as we assess each new role against another ethical principle, we can refine and further define what constitutes ethical professional behavior. Let us move now to the role of student development educator and assess the various subroles against our five principles.

The student development educator relates knowledge of theories and practices in learning and human development to all dimensions of student growth: intellectual, emotional, cultural, moral, physical, and interpersonal (Brown, 1980). He or she works with students and those who interact with students to assess developmental needs, helps to design and implement appropriate experiences to promote development, and evaluates progress. The student development educator can be witnessed in virtually every student services position. The work roles representing this model are those of adviser, instructor, program planner, researcher, and mentor. Table 2 relates examples of responsibilities for the five educator roles to the five ethical principles. We will first discuss behaviors for the adviser role across the five ethical categories. Then the do no harm principle will be addressed as it affects the remaining educator roles.

Respecting Autonomy. Advising in student services is an important form of interaction in undergraduate education. (For a discussion of ethical principles in advisement in graduate education, see Brown and Krager, in press). The advising role occurs in admissions, residence halls, judicial affairs, student government, and campus activities and in academic advising for undeclared majors and for those who have not yet been assigned an adviser in their major. Two important premises influence the discussion of student services advising. First, the adviser is usually expected to have knowledge and experience that is of value to the student. Consequently, adviser counsel can have a great impact on student decision making. Second, as a developmental educator, the adviser seeks to promote student growth by facilitating student self-direction.

Autonomy is central to the advising process. Some students may not have enough information on which to base a decision, and others prefer direct guidance and an abundance of structure. How much freedom should the adviser allow a student to choose among specific courses or act in organizational positions? Leadership roles in such organizations as student government or student union boards are intended to be learning experiences, yet decisions made by a leader could cause serious setbacks both for the student and for others. Autonomy reminds the adviser to provide challenge and opportunity but to do so according to the abilities of the particular student concerned.

Doing No Harm. As it does in the case of the administrator, harm is more likely to result from adviser misunderstanding or lack of awareness than from malice. Encouraging students to move into positions of responsibility for which they are unprepared might cause harm. Not providing adequate training for those in new leadership positions or placing rigorous work expectations on students with heavy academic loads can also be damaging.

To avoid harm, the adviser needs to be aware of other demands in the student's life (academics, organizational membership, work commitment). The adviser should be sensitive to the student's competencies, assist the student in recognizing limitations, and encourage the student to assess personal strengths and weaknesses accurately.

Benefiting Others. Advisers work with students in settings rich with developmental opportunity. To most high school seniors, selecting a college and setting up the first semester is a new and stressful experience. Knowledge of their abilities, personal expectations, and the expectations of others all play a part in their decisions. Educators in admissions and advising have an opportunity to assist the process and encourage participation in campus activities that facilitate continuing growth. The student appointed to a judicial board may find his or her moral beliefs challenged and witness the complexities involved in judging the behavior of peers. Student government leaders can test management skills and confront the subtleties of political process. The principle of benefiting others includes promoting their personal growth. Organizational experiences are opportunities to teach process as well as specific content.

Being Just. Justice in advising includes being available, spending comparable amounts of time, and giving proportional if not equal attention to all students. Students themselves are not equal in their energy, potential, interests, or physical attractiveness. Some will provide bright and stimulating conversation. Others will not be so personable and energetic. Some may become familiar to the adviser as a result of recognition and reward, others through matters of discipline. How can proportionate treatment be judged? When does disportionate time and attention become unjust?

Adviser time and attention can promote significant growth in the students who receive it, and no one type of student should remain an educator's only focus. Fair treatment not only affects the recipients but is a potent and positive example for others. The adviser can demonstrate fairness through availability, objective appraisals of student performance, and encouragement of openness and tolerance. Attention should be given to identifying those factors that tend to evoke special and inappropriate treatment. Self-awareness can help diffuse their undesirable influence.

Being Faithful. The principle of being faithful is particularly relevant for the educator. Acts of kindness and of being fair will rarely make a lasting impression if those acts are inconsistent, conditional, or short-lived. A student organization will experience difficulties as well as successes. Can the adviser be counted on for support, representation, or even advocacy in times of crises? Does a student feel that there must be a problem in order to receive the adviser's attention?

The adviser is responsible for giving the student or student group the opportunity to learn and succeed. Advisers should remain supportive through difficulties, but they should also make it clear that a problem does not have to be the only basis of interaction. Promise keeping can be demonstrated by respecting the confidentiality of personal sharing and by honoring agreements made for information and referrals. Fidelity can be measured in behavior over time and also in consistency of word and deed.

Developmental Educator Roles and the Principle of Doing No Harm

The preceding discussion shows how the five ethical principles relate to the adviser role. The discussion that follows focuses on how the principle of doing no harm applies to the roles of instructor, program planner, researcher, and mentor.

Instructor. The instructor role emphasizes delivery and style of presentation. It is typically thought of as classroom teaching methodology; however, the student services educator may assume the role in credit and noncredit courses, in special programs and workshops, and in in-service education for professional and paraprofessional staff. To identify desired teaching behaviors, two general areas of instruction need to receive careful consideration: instructor communication skills and individual student needs.

Regardless of content, the meaning will be lost without planful presentation. Information can be clouded in rhetoric, and facts can be mixed with opinion. Responsibility in instruction requires providing each student with the optimal opportunity to learn. The educator must ask, Am I making this meaningful? Meaningfulness is using what makes sense to the specific learner. Consideration of individual needs may require an assessment of student entering skills, a sample of learning styles, and some personal background on the student. A premise for beginning teaching is know the learners. Then, do not just teach, teach to them.

Program Planner. The program planner represents the duties performed in choosing content and in designing programs. For student services educators, this includes interdisciplinary courses (that is, orientation, career planning, personal development), special programs and workshops (that is, assertiveness, communication skills, leadership, time and financial management), in-service programs (that is, job skills, personal and professional growth topics), and courses in academic disciplines (that is, psychology, student personnel, health, and recreation). The foremost objective of the designer is to ensure that the program makes it possible to acquire the necessary skills and knowledge. This requires familiarity with the content and with the learning audience. The educator can use some basic questions to focus planning. For example, is there a need for a personal development class? Who is to be reached? What areas within personal development are most suitable for that population? Should the focus be on basic skills or on more sophisticated self-exploration?

We often need to reach a diverse audience with a single program. New student orientation classes are sometimes provided as the introduction to an institution for all students. But, do the classes address the special circumstances of the transfer, the international student, and students of nontraditional age? In-service education is another important planning area. How do we justify the student worker or professional staff member who has not been adequately oriented or trained for his or her position? The planner works to avoid harm by assessing and meeting the need for programs and by incorporating appropriate and adequate content.

Researcher. There are always ethical considerations when scientific inquiry is applied to human participants. The decision to do research in itself is obligated by an ethical concern to extend knowledge for the sake of human betterment. Research efforts in student affairs include seeking new information of particular use to the institution, answering general questions concerning student and organizational development, using assessment methods to evaluate services, and teaching research skills through staff development and degree programs. Research conduct is addressed in professional codes and published guidelines (American Psychological Association, 1982), but where questions arise in particular research and guidelines are lacking, professionals must still be held accountable for their decisions.

To avoid harm the developmental educator strives to conduct all research according to ethical principles (that is, respect autonomy, benefit others, be just, and be faithful) and to model ethical research techniques for colleagues and students. He or she also assumes the responsibility to intervene if there is evidence of unethical research procedures by others and to teach ethical research procedures to students and staff providing assistance.

Mentor. The mentor role may overlap with other roles. In fact, mentors have been found to perform a variety of functions, including teacher, counselor, guide, sponsor, and exemplar (Levinson, 1978). Although the mentoring relationship is often described as similar to the advising relationship, it goes beyond traditional advising in two significant ways: First, mentoring places more emphasis on modeling. Second, mentoring includes an extended dialogue that spans six growth dimensions: personal identity and life-style, interpersonal skill, academic skills, esthetic awareness, physical fitness, and multicultural awareness (DeCoster and Brown, 1982).

Mentoring's broad range of influence and degree of impact make it especially vulnerable to causing harm. Formal programs incorporate training and implementation guidelines, but most mentoring relationships are informal, and the effects of informal relationships are left to those involved. To avoid doing harm, developmental educators need to recognize the value of the role and to be aware of its responsibilities. For example, to what degree should the mentor expect loyalty in return for guidance? Student autonomy will be usurped if allegiance is expected or demanded on every issue, and using staff and student loyalty to fight personal battles only models injustice. Perhaps more than any other educator role, the mentor needs a good understanding of the student or staff member as a person and the wisdom to work effectively for the welfare of others.

Conclusion

The framework offered in this chapter has applied ethical principles to an analysis of administrator and educator work roles. Both the matrices and the discussion describe specific behavioral expectations for the practitioner. These examples were illustrative, not prescriptive.

The matrix schema can assist in making concerns for ethical practice more explicit. Tables can be designed for other areas of practice, such as the work roles of the counselor, the functions of a specific division, and the duties of an individual job description, and they can offer sample behaviors for each principle. The resulting schemas then provide a format for discussion based on a common ground, a common direction, and an emphasis on actual behaviors. The framework concept should facilitate the open discussion needed to define and incorporate ethical behavior into daily practice.

References

Ambler, D. A. "The Administrator Role." In U. Delworth and G. R. Hanson (Eds.), *Student Services: A Handbook for the Profession.* San Francisco: Jossey-Bass, 1980.

American Psychological Association. *Ethical Principles in the Conduct of Research with Human Participants.* Washington D. C.: American Psychological Association, 1982.

Brown, R. D. "Key Issues in Evaluating Student Affairs Programs." In G. Kuh (Ed.), *Evaluation in Student Affairs.* Cincinnati: American College Personnel Association, 1979.

Brown, R. D. "The Student Development Educator Role." In U. Delworth and G. R. Hansen (Eds.), *Student Services: A Handbook for the Profession.* San Francisco: Jossey-Bass, 1980.

Brown, R. D., and Krager, L. "Ethical Issues in Graduate Education: Faculty and Student Responsibilities." *Journal of Higher Education,* in press.

Canon, H. J. "Developing Staff Potential." In U. Delworth and G. R. Hanson (Eds.), *Student Services: A Handbook for the Profession.* San Francisco: Jossey-Bass, 1980.

DeCoster, D. A. and Brown, R. D. "Mentoring Relationships and the Educational Process." In R. D. Brown and D. A. DeCoster (Eds.), *Mentoring-Transcript Systems for Promoting Student Growth.* New Directions for Student Services, no. 19. San Francisco: Jossey-Bass, 1982.

Dutton, T. B., and Rickard, S. T. "Organizing Student Services." In U. Delworth and

G. R. Hanson (Eds.), *Student Services: A Handbook for the Profession.* San Francisco: Jossey-Bass, 1980.

Levinson, D. J. *The Seasons of a Man's Life.* New York: Knopf, 1978.

Richman, B. M., and Farmer, R. N. *Leadership, Goals, and Power in Higher Education: A Contingency and Open-Systems Approach to Effective Management.* San Francisco: Jossey-Bass, 1974.

LuAnn Krager is a staff member in the Division of Student Affairs at the University of Nebraska–Lincoln. She is a regular contributor to program presentations at conventions of the American College Personnel Association, and she has a sustained interest in professional ethics and in organizational systems.

Ethical standards statements are essential if the student affairs field is to consider itself a profession, but the adoption of standards statements alone does not assure ethical practice in the field.

Ethical Standards Statements: Uses and Limitations

Roger B. Winston, Jr.
John C. Dagley

Codes of ethics or statements of ethical standards have meaning in three contexts: philosophical, anthropological and psychological, and professional. The study of the rightness or wrongness, the goodness or badness of actions and of the justifications for such judgments is the traditional province of philosophers. The philosopher's concern about professional ethical standards is not so much about the specific rules, as it is about the rational, logical, and metaphysical justifications for such rules. Anthropologists seek to document the rules of conduct in a given society and the social and political mechanisms that are used to enforce them; they have few concerns about whether the rules are intrinsically right. Psychologists are concerned about how individuals go about making moral decisions and value judgments, that is, about the emotional and mental processes that individuals follow in making decisions and judgments. Both anthropology and psychology as disciplines are interested in ethics only in a descriptive sense. Seen from the context of a profession, ethics is concerned with the content of the rules, with who has the right to make the rules, and with how the rules are to be interpreted and enforced (Winston and McCaffrey, 1983). Many sociologists have argued that the existence of an enforceable code of ethics is at the very core of what it means to be a profession (Wilensky, 1964; Moore, 1970). This chapter identifies the purposes, uses, and limitations of ethical standards statements relevant to student affairs practice and discusses the development, scope, content, and enforcement of their provisions.

Codes of Professional Ethics: Purposes and Uses

Statements of ethical and professional standards serve seven purposes: as a concise statement of ideals that can instruct students preparing to enter the field, as guidelines that practitioners can use in making practical decisions, as a means of clarifying practitioners' responsibilities, as protection for the profession against unscrupulous persons, as assurance to the general public that practitioners will honor the values and accepted practices of the profession, as safeguards for practitioners when their integrity and performance are attacked, and as a basis for the appraisal and evaluation of performance (McGowan and Schmidt, 1962; Daniels, 1973; Loewenberg and Dolgoff, 1982; Winston and McCaffrey, 1983).

Pedagogical Tool. One of the most important uses of a code of ethics is to teach those preparing to enter the field about its ideals and to promote an awareness of the ethical implications of professional practice. During preparation students should become knowledgeable about the content of standards statements, but, even more important, they need to become sensitive to situations that have ethical implications and to processes for resolving ethical conflicts or dilemmas. Students need time to reflect on how they might deal with ethical problems before they encounter them. Once they are in a work setting, they often find that the press of time and circumstances can obscure important ethical and professional issues.

Guidelines for Practical Decisions. One of the primary reasons for having a code of professional ethics is to shift some of the responsibility for ethical decision making from the individual practitioner to the larger group or, more specifically, to the profession as embodied in a professional association. Ethical decisions and responsibility for such decisions may ultimately rest with the individual practitioner, but it is psychologically comforting to know that other responsible persons will support one's ethical stand. By devising ethical standards statements, the profession signifies its willingness to give moral support to practitioners when they face the ethical implications of their own and their colleagues' behaviors and to help them through the decision-making process. Codes also have practical utility, because they identify potential ethical problems and can thereby help practitioners to avoid unprofessional and unethical activities.

Any adequate decision-making process will include at least four steps: identification of the problem, specification of goals and objectives, generation and evaluation of alternative courses of action, and selection and implementation of a course of action. Van Hoose and Kottler (1977) and Winston and McCaffrey (1983) provide extended treatments of ethical decision making.

In step one, ethical standards statements lay the parameters of acceptable professional activity and identify the ideals and values upon which the profession is founded. Practitioners are not always aware that they are approaching ethically treacherous territory until it is too late. Ethical standards post danger signs. The more specific the standards statement, the more prominent are the danger signals.

Step two, specification of objectives, requires the examination of what one desires to have happen. After analyzing personal values and institutional and societal values and expectations, the professional must decide in step three whether to confront the ethical situation, attempt to avoid it, or pretend that it does not exist. If the professional decides to confront the ethical implications of the situation, then ethical standards statements can suggest guiding principles and strategies for step four, selecting and implementing a course of action. The more specific and detailed the code, the more support professionals will feel as they contemplate action; it allows professionals to show others that a respected and disinterested body has determined that a particular action is professionally or ethically inappropriate. However, standards statements cannot address all possible situations. Consequently, ethical codes need to strike a balance between broad ethical principles and the wide array of situations that practitioners will encounter. Most practitioners who seek answers to practical questions will view ethical codes composed only of general principles as platitudes that have little functional value. Specific guidelines set the boundaries of alternative actions and serve as reality anchors for the general principles and statements of values.

In step four, ethical codes may offer assistance in projecting possible consequences of actions. Generally, however, it is the individual practitioner who must select a course of action and summon the courage to follow it through. There is no substitute for individual responsibility and professional integrity. No written code can assure this.

Clarification of Responsibilities. If student affairs is to become a profession, then the field must be rigorous in assuring that each practitioner possesses the competence needed to perform the functions assigned. If a profession is to deserve the social status that society accords to professionals, it must take steps to protect clients from unprofessional or incompetent practitioners. Specifying the need for specialized preparation and continuing education, representing qualifications and experiences accurately, supporting the legitimate professional endeavors of colleagues, and supporting the missions of the institution at which they are employed are all examples of strictures that commonly appear in ethical standards and that serve to assure competent performance.

Protection of the Profession. As Mueller (1983, p. 191) observed about professionals nearly twenty-five years ago, "it is their altruism, their dedication to the general welfare, which gives the professionals their high standing in society, and it is their voluntary self-regulation which is essential to our democratic way of life. If they fail us even a little bit. . . . either in their skills or insights or in their will to work for our welfare, the public is quick to complain, exhort, vilify, and strike back." Ethical standards statements assist the members of a profession to maintain their vigilance in identifying and confronting colleagues who fail to meet their obligations. In effect, it sensitizes professionals to critical issues in daily practice. Standards statements help to assure that practitioners speak the same language and share some common expectations of each other as well.

Public Affirmation. Standards statements serve to explain to the public the role and function of student affairs in higher education—something the profession has always had a difficult time doing. They also assure the public that students' best interests will be the primary concern of professionals. As Section B—11 of the American College Personnel Association (1981) standards indicates, "members demonstrate sensible regard for the social codes and moral expectations of the communities in which they live and work." This does not mean that they must adopt any particular value orientation, lifestyle, or religious dogma. Rather, professionals can reasonably be expected to moderate their life-styles to to assure that their behavior outside the work setting does not adversely affect their capacity to function effectively within the institution. Professionals must be aware that the public views them as exemplars of the profession in everything they do, on and off campus.

A continuing source of conflict for many professionals involves the weighing of interests of individual students and staff members against the interests of the institution and society. Student affairs professionals have responsibilities both to individuals and to the institution. An adequate ethical code provides guidelines that professionals can use when they must make difficult decisions.

Protection of Individual Practitioners. One important aspect of a profession is that members support and defend one another when unjustly attacked. In order for this function not to become self-serving guildism, it is important for members to be able to ascertain what is appropriate behavior for professionals. Individual practitioners need clear statements that they can use to protect their own personal integrity and personal privacy. Student affairs staff are sometimes requested by institutional leaders to perform duties or tasks that are inappropriate. Unless staff members have a clear statement with which they can demonstrate that the profession deems an activity inappropriate, refusal can easily be interpreted as insubordination, indolence, or petulance. For example, it has been argued that an important role for student affairs staff is that of student advocate. Such a role can be unpopular with various constituencies within an institution; ethical codes can provide effective defense when we have to take unpopular positions.

Performance Appraisal. Just as standards statements can be used to defend individual actions within an institution, they can also be used to define what activities should be evaluated and how that evaluation is to be accomplished. Student affairs can exist only within a institution, which is a basically bureaucratic organization; thus, it is important for the evaluation criteria employed to respect the autonomy and integrity of the profession. Ethical codes can be a source of such criteria. The work of the Council for the Advancement of Standards for Student Services/Development Programs will provide more comprehensive and detailed guidance than we now possess (Mable and Miller, 1983). However, until such time as those standards are available, codes of ethics must fufill this role.

Etiology of Ethical Standards

Emerging professions confront several issues and choices in the pursuit of ethical standards. One of the first tasks that a professional association encounters is the selection of a process for developing a code of ethics. Typically, professions have used one or more of the following approaches: empirical or quasi-empirical approaches, which can be divided into two categories—critical incident analysis and delphi consensus seeking—and nonempirical approaches, which can be approached through moral or philosophical analysis, legal issues and concerns, adaption/adoption, normative consensus judgment, and analysis of complaints.

Student affairs professionals have been characterized as pragmatic doers who are not particularly drawn to abstract analysis. Evidence of this practical bent is apparent in the approaches to the development of ethical standards taken by the various student affairs-related professional associations. Most groups have appointed and charged committees to draft general ethical statements for consideration, revision, and adoption by the general membership. While it is virtually impossible at this point to determine clearly the primary motives underlying the actions of these early committees, it seems that there are at least two goals: to develop a base of consensual agreement regarding the profession's guiding principles and dominant values and to establish professional identity—to take that one additional step toward achieving the status of a profession. Regardless of specific purposes, the associations have generally opted for direct and practical approaches to standards development rather than for such indirect and abstract approaches as in-depth analysis of philosophical beliefs and assumptions.

The American College Personnel Association (ACPA) used a combination of the approaches just described in its first effort to develop a code through adaption of the American Personnel and Guidance Association (APGA) ethical standards. An early ACPA task force analyzed the APGA standards and proposed a list of broad philosophical principles that the Executive Council rejected as lacking the desired specificity. A new task force was named. It used a more empirical approach—a modified delphi technique—to develop its present statement. Modifications of the statement were made through three rounds of input from executive council members, commission chairpersons, and state division presidents; open hearings; and written input from members at large. The resulting statement (American College Personnel Association, 1981) is therefore an example of the quasi-empirical approach to development.

Other associations have used different methods. For example, the American Psychological Association (APA) developed its first statement of ethical standards by going directly to its members for initial input: In 1948, members "were asked by letter to describe from firsthand knowledge a situation in which a psychologist made a decision having ethical implications and to indicate what the correspondent perceived as being the ethical issue involved" (Golann, 1970, p. 400). The resulting empirically derived code reflected the daily experiences of a representative group of practitioners. While the set of standards has been modified over the years, the original critical incident approach yielded specific cases that served as guidelines for three years, after which time more general principles were written.

Scope of Standards

Another set of questions that an emerging profession, such as student affairs, encounters has to do with the desired level of comprehensiveness and specificity of the statements. How detailed should standards statements be? These questions help to explain the wide range of differences in current ethical standards statements. As Table 1 shows, there is a great deal of overlap among the general content areas. Specificity is determined not only by major categories but also by the way in which the standards are written and supported. In fact, a code can be considered quite general when viewed by category, but when the category is described with specific examples, it would be considered quite specific. For instance, the APA's (1981) *Speciality Guidelines for Delivery of Services by Counseling Psychologists* consists of four broad categories: providers, programs, accountability, and environment. However, each of these four areas is broken down into component parts, with specific "interpretations" and case comments included for each. At the other end of the continuum is the general responsibilities statement of the National Association of Women Deans, Administrators, and Counselors (NAWDAC) (1976); one of its thirteen statements says (p. 80) that it is the responsibility of educators to "conduct a continuing review of described responsibilities and seek ways to improve the existing professional climate."

It is interesting to note the differences in specificity of two different codes when dealing with the same or with similar issues. For example, section B-12 of the ACPA's (1981) standards states that "Members maintain ethical relationships with colleagues and students and refrain from relationships which impinge on the dignity, moral code, self-worth, professional functioning, and/or personal growth of these individuals. Specifically, members are aware that sexual relationships hold great potential for exploitation. Consequently, members refrain from having sexual relationships with anyone to whom they act as counselors or therapists. Sexual relationships with staff

Table 1. Comparative Analysis of Statements of Ethical Standards of Selected Professional Associations

Content	Student-Affairs Related Professional Associations					
	ACPA	ACUHO	APA	AACD (APGA)	NASPA	NAWDAC
Relationships						
Students	A	C	B	B	C	D
Professionals	A	C	A	B	C	C
Institutional	A	C	B	B	C	C
Counseling	B	D	B	A	D	D
Supervisory	A	C	B	B	C	D
Instructional	B	C	B	A	D	D
Research and Testing						
Research and Publication	A	C	A	A	C	D
Measurement	B	D	B	A	D	D
Functional Issues						
Competence	A	C	A	B	C	C
Communications with Public	B	C	A	B	C	D
Confidentiality	B	C	B	B	C	D
Consultation/Referrals	C	C	B	A	D	D
Moral and Legal	B	D	B	B	C	D
Nondiscrimination	A	D	A	A	C	D
Resource management	D	C	D	D	C	C
Evaluation (program and personnel)	A	C	C	C	C	C
Employment practices	A	D	D	D	C	B
Professional preparation	A	D	C	A	D	D
Enforcement of Standards	D	D	B	B	D	C

A = Standards statement makes a clear and comprehensive statement of expected behavior and includes explanatory materials or examples.
B = Standards state broad principles.
C = Standards briefly, indirectly, or somewhat unclearly address the issues.
D = Standards do not address issues.

ACPA = American College Personnel Association
ACUHO = Association of College and University Housing Officers
APA = American Psychological Association
AACD = American Association of Counseling and Development (formerly American Personnel and Guidance Association)
NASPA = National Association of Student Personnel Administrators
NAWDAC = National Association of Women Deans, Administrators, and Counselors

members or students for whom one has supervisory or evaluative responsibilities have high potential for causing personal damage and for limiting the exercise of professional responsibilities and are therefore unprofessional and unethical." On the same sugject, section A-8 of the AACD ethical standards (Callis and others, 1982, p. 10) states that "In the counseling relationship the counselor is aware of the intimacy of the relationship and maintains respect for the client and avoids engaging in activities that seek to meet the counselor's personal needs at the expense of that client. Through awareness of the negative impact of both racial and sexual stereotyping and discrimination, the counselor guards the individual rights and personal dignity of the client in the counseling relationship."

Codes of ethical standards also differ in the scope and nature of coverage. The ACPA's standards are rather comprehensive, concentrating on responsibility, competency, research, and relationships. The most attractive feature of the ACPA standards is the level of specificity, particularly in difficult areas. The example just given reflects the ACPA approach to providing guidance for problem areas. The standards statements of the NAWDAC (1976) and the American Association of University Administrators (AAUA) (Hollander, 1980) are distinct in their emphasis on the rights of professionals, although both sets of standards tend to be restricted to the rights of employees. Nevertheless, by emphasizing the rights of professionals, these standards indirectly serve to protect the integrity of both the individual and the services and programs provided to students.

Nature of the Content

A third issue consists of decisions about the nature of the actual content of the ethical statements. Should the statements deal with controversial issues, such as employment of homosexual staff members or admission of marginally prepared students without providing adequate academic and psychological support services, or should they not?

The standards compared in Table 1 are representative but by no means exhaustive of the student affairs organizations that have developed ethical standards statements. While there are obvious similarities among the codes compared here, there are also some marked contrasts. For example, there seems to be a true difference of opinion on the issue of the object of the member's primary responsibility. The AACD (1981, section B-1) states: "The member's primary obligation is to respect the integrity and promote the welfare of the client(s)." At the other end of the continuum is the NASPA (1983, section 5) statement: "Members recognize that their primary obligation is to the employing institution." While this statement is made in the context of conflict of interests, the NASPA statement seems to emphasize concern for the institution over the interests of individuals. Somewhere between these two positions is the ACPA (1981, section D-5) statement: "Members have responsibilities both to the individuals served and to the institution within which the service is performed." By seeking the middle ground, the ACPA creates ambiguity for those who are seeking guidance in making practical decisions. How does one satisfy conflicting interests? None of the ethical standards reviewed answers that question. The reason may be that there is an inherent conflict in student affairs practice, because the profession is emerging within a bureaucracy.

Student Affairs as a Profession in a Bureaucracy

The traditional view of professions is based on the models of law, medicine, and the clergy, which once included university faculty. The first two professions have the potential to function alone outside any institution or bureaucracy. The church, and later the universities when they split away, have traditionally been relatively complex organizations. The conventional conceptions of professions and bureaucracies conflict, because they are founded on different principles of organization. Professional work has had as its ideal the craftsman; that is, all operations needed to produce the final product are performed by one person, possibly assisted by apprentices. In contrast, bureaucracies have been organized on the principle that tasks can be divided into constituent activities and that individuals or groups of workers need to know how to perform only a limited number of tasks. The workers do not need to understand the overall operation; there are people — administrators — within the organization whose function is to oversee operations and coordinate the efforts of others. From this perspective, higher education institutions are bureaucracies. The existence of student affairs as a separate entity denotes a division of responsibilities between in-class and outside-of-class education of students; academic colleges within universities, departments within colleges, and specialized programs and areas within departments all bespeak the compartmentalization of American higher education (Mendenhall and others, 1983).

Scott (1966) identified four areas of conflicts for professionals in organizations: resistance to bureaucratic rules, rejection of bureaucratic standards, resistence to supervision, and conditional loyalty to the organization.

Professionals possess extensive skills and knowledge that equip them to operate at a very sophisticated level and an ideology that defines the purpose of their work. The commonly simplistic nature of bureaucratic rules almost inevitably leads to conflict with the high level of complexity and sophistication. If the ideal of student affairs practice is to assist each student in realizing his or her potential to the fullest, as "The Student Personnel Point of View" (1983) states, then there is bound to be conflict with the organization when its leadership decides that curbs must be placed on some exercise of activity. The era of student unrest in the 1960s produced considerable conflict for many student affairs practitioners when college administrations began to curtail demonstrations and other acts of protest. The question was often asked, Who are the clients—the institutional leaders or the students? The control of student behavior function has traditionally been assigned to student affairs, but it has also often been an area of disagreement with institutional leaders.

For student affairs professionals, the second area of conflict, resistance to bureaucratic standards, generally centers on disagreement about the goals of student development. If student affairs divisions see their goal as making an important contribution to the education of students and if the institutional authorities see it as exercising control over student behavior and providing ancillary support services, then conflict is bound to ensue, because preparation programs espouse an educational goal for the profession, and professional associations exhort student development concepts—both external to the bureaucracy. Ethical standards statements extol the educational function for student affairs.

The third area of conflict, resistance to bureaucratic supervision, stems from the fact that authority is created by position in the bureaucracy, not by the knowledge and experience of those who hold the positions. For example, many college presidents assume their position without an understanding of or experience in student affairs. Struggles often ensue simply because the top administrator does not understand or does not value the mission that student affairs professionals set for themselves.

The fourth area of conflict for professionals, conditional loyalty to the bureaucracy, also produces strains. As Scott (1966) notes, professionals who have completed a training program that provides practitioners with standards and norms independent of any particular organization often come to develop a professional self-image, in the sense that they value their skills highly and that they are concerned more with getting and maintaining a reputation among peers than with pleasing organizational superiors. Their identification is not with the particular institution but with the student affairs professions.

Ethical standards statements in student affairs can both promote professionalization of the field and help to diminish the conflicts that practitioners experience within their employing institutions. Standards statements can alert professionals to potential conflict areas, which they may seek to resolve with institutional leaders before a crisis arises, and they can provide guidance to professionals concerning legitimate obligations and duties to one's employer. Student affairs practitioners will always have two client constituencies—individual students and student groups on the one hand and institutions on the other.

The existence of these client constituencies for student affairs is reflected in the distinct differences among the statements in the area of relationships. As Table 1 shows, the ACPA statement about personal and professional relationships is the most extensive and speciffc. At the other end, the NAWDAC's (1976, p. 79) expectation that a member will "conduct her/his professional activities in accord with the institution's stated objectives and policies and in a manner that maintains and perpetuates institutional and personal relationships of mutual trust and openness" is the epitome of generality.

The statement of each professional association reflects its character and orientation. For example, the AACD, ACPA and APA standards on research and testing are clear and comprehensive, while the NASPA and NAWDAC statements barely mention responsibilities associated with research, publication, testing, and measurement, although they do emphasize employee obligations and institutional priorities.

Few areas of ethical responsibility are given equal treatment by the associations whose standards are compared in Table 1. Professional competence, professional and institutional relationships, and confidentiality are the only areas on which all the standards statements touch. However, even in these areas, there are varying levels of emphasis. For instance, regarding confidentiality, the NASPA statement focuses on the necessity of keeping confidential institutional records, while the other codes view confidentiality more in terms of relationships with students and staff and of privileged communication. In another area, the Association of College and University Housing Officers (ACUHO), the NASPA, and the NAWDAC are the only associations that directly address the management of resources. Budgeting within the context of ethical principles and fiscal responsibility seem to be more significant issues for these groups than they are for the AACD, the ACPA, and the APA. Standards for professional preparation are included only in the ACPA and AACD statements. This benign neglect may reflect, or at least explain, the somewhat distant relationships (and in some cases the indifference) found on some university campuses between student personnel preparation programs and student affairs professionals and programs.

Limitations of Current Ethical Standard Statements

Student affairs–related professional associations have initiated commendable efforts to develop functional statements of professional ethics. The next state of development undoubtedly will witness specific steps to address some of the limitations noted here.

Enforcement of standards often sets up adversarial postures resembling those found in the legal system. While it is essential for alleged violators to be confronted and to be accorded a fair opportunity to respond, the emphasis should be placed on fostering ethical conduct among professionals and the institutions in which they work, not on holding elaborate hearings or on meting out penalties.

Most statements are reactive in nature. They fail to mandate opposition to institutional practices that are not developmentally sound, such as requiring all students to declare a major at the time of enrollment or creating policy that tells students what to do, not situations that allow students to become more cognitively complex by confronting important problems. They also fail to mandate advocacy of the integration of developmental learning experiences inside and outside the classroom, that is, student development.

Statements tend to assume idealized working conditions and institutional leadership. For instance, they generally say that professionals should attempt to settle ethical problems within institutional channels before involving persons from outside, but most colleges do not have systematic procedures for dealing with ethical issues and disagreements.

Institutions and professionals have generally failed to use standards statements for developing policies that could prevent foreseeable ethical problems. For example, many institutions avoid making policy statements or intentionally formulate ambiguous statements in order to avoid politically or emotionally charged situations. However, the result is inappropriate decisions for which the institution becomes responsible or for which individual practitioners are singled out for ridicule or censure. Moreover, standards statements generally have failed to anticipate new areas of ethical conflict or problems that technical advances, such as use of computers and biofeedback, can cause.

Many standards statements have built-in conflicts or inconsistencies. While it is probably impossible to eliminate all internal inconsistencies, means should be provided to guide users in resolving conflicting mandates or principles. Consequently, detailed casebooks or other means of identifying specific appropriate and inappropriate behaviors are essential to understanding the implications of any standards statements. Finally, most professional associations lack workable mechanisms for assuring compliance with their ethical standards statements. In fact, most student affairs–related associations make no provisions for providing consultation, monitoring, or enforcement of standards.

Monitoring and Enforcing Compliance with Standards

Statements of ethical standards seem to mature in distinct stages. Typically, when a profession recognizes the need for a statement, it commissions a group of its members to outline general ethical guidelines; the result is then submitted to the membership in one form or another for adaptation or adoption. Next, a committee is charged to follow experimental use of the statement for several years in order to determine its utility and validity. The ethical standards of student affairs professional associations are for the most part now at this stage of development. However, some have progressed to the point of using an empirical process to revise the original code or to start anew. As each stage is accomplished, the level of specificity and the scope of coverage increases. Professional associations then embark on extensive educational programs, using case studies in comprehensive casebooks (Callis and others, 1982; American Psychological Association, 1967) whenever possible, to clarify the specific content of the ethics statements. The final stage—it has proved to be somewhat elusive for all professions—involves the development and implementation of an effective monitoring and enforcement system.

If codes of ethics do not include monitoring and enforcement mechanisms, there is some question as to their usefulness. As Schurr (1982, p. 332) notes, "a code is but a pious fraud if it is unenforceable. There must be some form of due process for the resolution of disputes." Broad principles of desired personal and professional conduct can sound pious and platitudinous unless they are accompanied by descriptive material that anchors the principles in behavior.

The AACD and the APA have both procedures in place for investigating and adjudicating alleged violations of their ethical standards. The AACD has two procedures—one for members accusing members of violations and another for nonmembers accusing members. The APA uses the same process no matter who brings the charges.

AACD Member Allegations of Violations. The AACD (Callis and others, 1982) has developed an enforcement process to monitor the professional conduct of its members so as to assure ethical practice. Its policies and procedures for the confidential processing of complaints about ethical violations become operational with the receipt of a complaint about the conduct of a member. Once the AACD membership of the accused and the complainant have been established, AACD staff members notify the Ethics Committee chairperson, the complainant, and the accused that action is pending. Simultaneously, the AACD secures a legal opinion about the legitimacy of the complaint. To facilitate the implementation of these initial steps, the AACD requires the complainant, first, to consult a colleague to seek another opinion about whether ethical standards have been breached; second, to attempt to resolve the dispute directly with the accused; third, to contact the president of the AACD state branch to determine the feasibility of handling the matter at the state level; and fourth, to submit a formal, written statement of the alleged violations (witnessed by an AACD member) to the Ethics Committee chairperson.

Among other immediate tasks, the Ethics Committee chairperson informs the accused of the specific accusations and requests a response within thirty days. Next, the chairperson develops a plan for investigating the charges. The accused is notified of his or her rights to a formal hearing before the full committee. Hearings are held with both the accused and the complainant in attendance, along with witnesses for all parties. The parties involved must pay expenses for themselves, witnesses, and legal counsel (who may be retained to serve as advisers). The burden of proof rests with the complainant.

Once the investigation has been completed, including the hearing if requested, the Ethics Committee notifies all parties of its decision. Both the complainant and the accused are advised of the appeals process, which entails a review by a three-person committee composed of high association officers.

Nonmember Allegations of Violations. Procedures for handling accusations from nonmembers—ordinarily members' clients—follow a different procedure. Nonmember complainants are asked to write to the chairperson of the AACD state branch ethics committee outlining the specific allegations. The state committee is expected to deal with the case in accordance with its own procedures. If deemed appropriate, the state branch ethics committee may refer the case to the AACD Ethics Committee.

AACD Sanctions Against Members. The Ethics Committee has several options for action available when violations have been established: issuance of a reprimand, withdrawal of membership for a specified period of time, probation, expulsion, and notification of appropriate certification and licensure boards about violations.

APA Enforcement Processes. The American Psychological Association has a monitoring and enforcement mechanism that has been operational for decades. Its Committee on Scientific and Professional Ethics and Conduct is charged to protect the public against harmful conduct by psychologists and to take action against members who are found to be guilty of misconduct that is educative and constructive in nature, not punitive.

The APA committee functions somewhat like the AACD ethics committee. However, it serves more as a fact-finding body, deciding along with the administrative officers whether to present a formal charge to the APA's president, at which time the accused can request a formal hearing. The president appoints three members of a twelve-member standing hearing panel to serve as the hearing committee. Two other differences between the policies and procedures of the APA and the AACD are apparent. First, the APA handles complaints from members and nonmembers in the same fashion. Second, the APA's national ethics committee decides whether to involve state or regional associations.

APA Sanctions Against Violators. The sanctions available to the APA's committee are similar to those of the AACD. The committee can request the member to cease the challenged conduct; it can issue a statement of censure and reprimand; it can require supervision, rehabilitation, education, or psychotherapy; it can place the member on probation for purposes of monitoring; it can allow the member to resign under stipulated conditions; it can refer to a state or regional psychological association, a state board of examiners, or both for action; and it can expel the member from the association.

Cases considered by the APA's committee in 1983 resulted in actions that represented most of the options just named. According to the committee's 1983 annual report (Webb, 1984), approximately three fourths of the cases acted upon were closed with no sanctions, reprimands, or censures. Approximately four months were required to adjudicate cases in 1983. Finally, categorization of cases by type of alleged misconduct reveals that charges concerning sexual intimacy, sexual harassment, and fraudulent claims or exorbitant fees increased dramatically from 1982.

Both the AACD's and the APA's approaches have serious limitations. First, all the options are adversarial in nature, rather than cooperative efforts at problem solving. Hearings are held at which the complainant confronts the accused. Usually, the association does not pay expenses for anyone other than its own committee, which places the burden on the complainant and witnesses. Further, fact-finding efforts are not very apparent or professional. Association membership and expulsion seem to be the ultimate weapons in the arsenals of the professions; thus, their effectiveness in dealing with alleged unethical behavior is severely limited.

Mediation Approach to Ethical Problems

The American Association of University Administrators (AAUA) offers student affairs professionals an attractive alternative to the adversarial approaches to enforcement. The AAUA uses a mediation approach to resolving conflict in higher education (Hollander, 1980). As an advocate of its professional standards for administrators in higher education (American Association of University Administrators, 1981), which specifies rights and responsibilities for members and employing institutions, the AAUA undertakes cases that afford an opportunity to resolve conflicts through amicable solutions. The AAUA uses no sanctions or blacklisting arrangements against either individuals or institutions, since it sees its role as advisory and constructive. The mediation procedures involve a three-step process involving inquiry, visitation, and review. The approach taps the expertise of volunteer administrators, a team purposively composed of individuals professionally similar to the disputing parties, to bring individuals and institutions together, without publicity, to work out possible resolutions. The process is not mystical, just hard work. Thus far, the AAUA has found one of the most pleasant results of the process to be the changing of institutional policy and procedures (Hollander, 1980).

This approach seems ideal for situations that involve employment disputes, but it seems to hold less promise for areas that affect the role and function of a student affairs division and its members. However, student affairs associations should consider adding this approach to their repertory of mechanisms for encouraging ethical behavior, especially since they now have no mechanisms for dealing with institutions.

Conclusion

The student affairs field has made considerable progress over the last decade in coming to grips with the responsibilities of an emerging profession. Increasing attention to ethical standards and their enforcement is a sign that the field is reaching maturity. While formal ethical standards are important and helpful, they generally are useful only when the problem has a superior or clearly right solution; ethical standards can help to give professionals backbone. In situations where all the alternatives seem to be equally good or bad or where the ethical principles within a statement conflict, ethical standards have limited value. Ultimately, ethical professional behavior rests on the personal integrity of individual students affairs professionals and on their commitment to the values and ideals of the profession. However, professional associations should support individuals by promulgating ethical standards that are specific enough to guide daily activities and by supporting and encouraging practitioners who are willing to confront unethical practices by individuals and institutions. At the very least, professional associations should assume responsibility for sending all new members a standards statement and for publishing adopted standards in professional journals where they will remain accessible to all who are interested long after initial adoption.

As of 1984, the student affairs profession has a number of statements of ethical and professional standards, but for the most part it lacks effective enforcement or sanctioning procedures. Only the AACD has specified procedures for addressing complaints of violations, but its standards statement focuses primarily on concerns associated with counseling practice.

While the student affairs field has made substantial progress in moving toward the status of a profession (Carpenter and others, 1980), there is still a pressing need to develop a comprehensive statement of ethical standards, endorsable by most practitioners, that includes a procedure for investigating alleged violations and for applying either mediation or sanctions procedures when violations are substantiated.

References

American Association of University Administrators. "Professional Standards for Administrators." In R. H. Stein and M. C. Baca (Eds.), *Professional Ethics in University Administration.* New Directions for Higher Education, no. 33. San Francisco: Jossey-Bass, 1981.

American College Personnel Association. "Statement of Ethical and Professional Standards." *Journal of College Student Personnel,* 1981, *42,* 184-189.

American Psychological Association. *Casebook on Ethical Standards of Psychologists.* Washington, D. C.: American Psychological Association, 1967.

American Psychological Association. *Speciality Guidelines for the Delivery of Services by Counseling Psychologists.* Washington, D. C.: American Psychological Association, 1981.

Callis, R., Pope, S. K., and DePauw, M. E. *APGA Ethical Standards Casebook.* (3rd ed.) Falls Church, Va.: American Personnel and Guidance Association, 1982.

Carpenter, D. S., Miller, T. K., and Winston, R. B., Jr. "Towards the Professionalization of Student Affairs." *NASPA Journal,* 1980, *18* (2), 16-22.

Daniels, A. K. "How Free Should Professions Be?" In E. Friedson (Ed.), *The Professions and Their Prospects.* Beverly Hills, Calif.: Sage, 1973.

Golann, S. E. "Ethical Standards for Psychology: Development and Revision, 1938-1968." *Annals of the New York Academy of Sciences,* 1970, *169,* 398-405.

Hollander. P. A. "A Mediation Service for Administrators Regarding AAUA Standards." In J. McCarthy (Ed.), *Resolving Conflict in Higher Education.* New Directions for Higher Education, no. 32. San Francisco: Jossey-Bass, 1980.

Loewenberg, F., and Dolgoff, R. *Ethical Decisions for Social Work Practice.* Itasca, Ill.: Peacock, 1982.

Mable, P., and Miller, T. K. "Standards for Professional Practice." In T. K. Miller, R. B. Winston, Jr., and W. R. Mendenhall (Eds.), *Administration and Leadership in Student*

Affairs: Actualizing Student Development in Higher Education. Muncie, Ind.: Accelerated Development, 1983.

McGowan, J. F., and Schmidt, L. D. (Eds.). *Counseling: Readings in Theory and Practice.* New York: Holt, Rinehart and Winston, 1962.

Mendenhall, W. R., Miller, T. K., and Winston, R. B., Jr. "Roles and Functions of Student Affairs Professionals." In T. K. Miller, R. B. Winston, Jr., and W. R. Mendenhall (Eds.), *Administration and Leadership in Student Affairs: Actualizing Student Development in Higher Education.* Muncie, Ind.: Accelerated Development, 1983.

Moore, W. E. *The Professions: Roles and Rules.* New York: Russell Sage Foundation, 1970.

Mueller, K. H. "The Professional as an Individual." In B. A. Belson and L. E. Fitzgerald (Eds.), *Thus, We Spoke: ACAA-NAWDAC, 1958-1975.* Carbondale, Ill.: American College Personnel Association, 1983.

National Association of Student Personnel Administrators. "NASPA Standards of Professional Practice." Unpublished document approved by NASPA Executive Committee, February 1983.

National Association of Women Deans, Administrators, and Counselors. "NAWDAC Statement of Principles, Purposes and Professional Standards of Conduct." Unpublished document approved by NAWDAC business meeting, March 20, 1976.

Schurr, G. M. "Toward a Code of Ethics for Academics." *Journal of Higher Education,* 1982, *53,* 318-334.

Scott, W. R. "Professionals in Bureaucracies—Areas of Conflict." In H. M. Vollmer and D. L. Mills (Eds.), *Professionalization.* Englewood Cliffs, N. J.: Prentice-Hall, 1966.

"The Student Personnel Point of View." In G. L. Saddlemire and A. L. Rentz (Eds.), *Student Affairs—A Profession's Heritage: Significant Articles, Authors, Issues, and Documents.* Carbondale, Ill.: American College Personnel Association, 1983.

Van Hoose, W. H., and Kottler, J. A. *Ethical and Legal Issues in Counseling and Psychotherapy.* San Francisco: Jossey-Bass, 1977.

Webb, W. B. *Annual Report of the Committee on Scientific and Professional Ethics and Conduct, 1983.* Report to the American Psychological Association, 1984.

Wilensky, H. L. "The Professionalization of Everyone?" *American Journal of Sociology,* 1964, *70,* 137-158.

Winston, R. B., Jr., and McCaffrey, S. S. "Ethical Practice in Student Affairs Administration." In T. K. Miller, R. B. Winston, Jr., and W. R. Mendenhall (Eds.), *Administration and Leadership in Student Affairs: Actualizing Student Development in Higher Education.* Muncie, Ind.: Accelerated Development, 1983.

Roger B. Winston, Jr., is associate professor in the Student Personnel in Higher Education Program, Department of Counseling and Human Development Services, University of Georgia. He chaired the ACPA task force that drafted the current ethical standards and serves on the ACPA Ethical and Professional Conduct Committee.

John C. Dagley is associate professor in the Student Personnel in Higher Education Program, Department of Counseling and Human Development Services Department, University of Georgia. He has served on panels that dealt with ethical dilemmas and issues at several state and national professional conferences.

Student affairs divisions have both an opportunity and an obligation to create an ethical campus community based on global as well as local perspectives.

Creating an Ethical Community

Robert D. Brown

What comes to mind when you hear the words, *professional ethics* or *ethical standards?* Several student affairs professionals wrote down anonymously a word or phrase in response to this question. Their answers included: "esoteric issues," "minimal expectations," "lots of *do nots,*" "irrelevant to me," and "issues for those who like semantics." How different are these responses from what you might hear from professional colleagues? Are ethical concerns for student affairs professionals minimal, narrow, negative, and applicable only to the clearly unethical and unprincipled? The authors of the preceding chapters suggest that they are not.

Canon shows in Chapter One how ethical dilemmas touch everyone in student affairs, and Kitchener in Chapter Two and Krager in Chapter Three demonstrate that ethical behavior requires action as well as reaction. Ethical behavior for student affairs professionals includes helping others as well as avoiding doing harm to others. In Chapter Four, Winston and Dagley trace the development of ethical standards and note that ethical behavior depends ultimately on the personal and professional integrity of individuals. Unlike the responses of student affairs professionals cited in the first paragraph, the authors of the chapters of this sourcebook characterize professional ethics as demanding, broad, positive, and applicable to all professionals. These conflicting perspectives suggest the need to reconsider how to think about ethical concerns.

This chapter proposes that it is the special mission of student affairs to be the conscience of the campus and explores how the concept of community provides a framework for establishing an ethical agenda, an action agenda. The chapter suggests why being the conscience of the campus is a possible role for student affairs. It examines how a community perspective is essential for defining the common good, and it describes the community perspectives that are important when developing an ethical agenda. It presents the implications of a community perspective on the planning of an ethical agenda, and it provides an illustrative checklist for establishing an ethical agenda for student affairs.

The Mission of Student Affairs

The unique mission of student services professionals can be difficult to discern. Because staff teach, counsel, work in housing, advise student organizations, and administer agencies and programs, they risk losing the communal character of our professional mission. They benefit greatly from the diversity of roles and campus locations, but they also risk being trapped by the need to cope with the daily crises within our particular professional spheres of interest. It is difficult to picture the whole. Student services becomes so specialized that is it difficult to envision its separate tasks as a common mission. What, then, is the common mission?

The common mission of the student services profession is being the moral conscience of the campus. Staff responsibility is to promote and support ethical behavior on campus and to recognize and confront unethical behavior. This mission is fulfilled by providing services and by creating a climate that facilitates student development, in particular the development of student values. Students' value systems are a complex configuration of how they respond to injustices, how they perceive their career goals, how they interact with other people, what they learn in the classroom, what life-styles they prefer, and what meaning they find in their own lives and in the lives of others. Student services is involved in each of these dimensions of a student's campus life through housing, advising, counseling, student activities, orientation, and discipline.

Higher education has never denied that its goal is to graduate responsible and ethical citizens as well as trained professionals and competent thinkers. At times, higher education has been frustrated by its inadequacies, and it has failed to recognize the interdependence between and the interactions among the dimensions of college life that promote students' intellectual, moral, and personal development. But, college catalogues continue to espouse the worth of personal development (Bowen, 1982).

Student affairs has greater potential to influence student values and to be the moral conscience of the campus that do faculty or other campus administrators. For the most part, faculty also support ethical development as a legitimate institutional goal, especially as it relates to development of the social consciousness expected of good citizens and as it encourages the ethical behavior expected of professionals. However, faculty also often find it difficult to remove the departmental and disciplinary blinders that limit their perspectives. They have difficulty seeing how the way in which they teach can make a difference; they more commonly focus on their own research and on the content of their discipline. The broad dimensions of student growth seem less pressing. Faculty are perhaps less disinterested in the personal development of students than they are distracted by the particular demands of their specific academic interests.

Campus administrators may be more likely to have a broad picture of student development than faculty do, but they, too, are distracted. They need to attend to other audiences, such as alumni, benefactors, parents, legislatures, and boards. They must respond to the concerns of faculty as well as to those of students. Administrative decisions are more public than those of the faculty, and their critics are often more vocal and powerful. In the midst of crises and budget talks, it is easy for administrators to misplace priorities.

The student services profession is in a unique position to promote student development and to be the conscience of the campus for several reasons. Unlike an academic department or college, student services as a collective entity is involved with the whole student. Student services staff are in contact with students where they live and eat, plan and play. Because of these contacts, they are aware of student indiscretions across a wide sphere of campus activities that range from cheating in the classroom to drug use in the residence halls. They are also aware of injustices visited on students by other students, faculty, and administrators.

Even more important than the contacts with students in the many facets of student life is the commitment that the student affairs profession has made to student development. This commitment provides a cohesive base for a common mission. It has been operationalized with support of and encouragement for research on student development and by design and implementation of campus policies and practices that are consistent with developmental goals and with what research and theory suggest will work.

The potential power of this common mission—being the conscience of the campus—is that by its uniqueness and visibility it can serve and inspire many more than those who are immediately affected. Recognition and continuing commitment to this communal mission are crucial both as student services professionals and as citizens of planet Earth.

A Community Perspective for an Ethical Agenda

The major thrust of this chapter is that the student services profession needs to establish an ethical agenda in order to fulfill its mission. This agenda needs to be derived from the perspective of a community of professionals.

Community is often defined as people living in the same locality. However, under a broader definition a community is a gathering of people with similar concerns and common goals who share a mutual interest in assisting or supporting one another. The term *community,* therefore, is not limited to people in the same town; it can also be used to describe people with similar interests and goals who manage to become aware of their commonalities and who provide one another with support. Thus, it is possible for professionals to form communities even when members are miles apart. They can share common concerns and goals and provide one another with intellectual and moral support.

Appropriate ethical behavior is often determined by relating it to what is thought to be the common good, which is usually influenced by community norms. The importance placed on community norms is influenced by the value placed on the communities to which individuals belong: neighborhood, church, organizations, state, country, work setting, or profession. When the norms of the different communities conflict, individuals are confronted with a dilemma. What is the common good for one community may not be the common good for another. Which community provides the norms?

Making decisions about ethical behavior in student services requires balancing what is good for the individual or group (for example, student, staff member, agency) and what is best for the common good (for example, all students, all staff members, all student affairs agencies). Should a student be permitted to break a residence hall lease because he or she is dissatisfied with the racial mixture? Should a senior staff member who has not grown professionally over the past few years be retained? Should a counseling director use a friendship relationship with the vice-president to seek additional staff when other agencies also have need for additional staff?

The common good in these examples may seem to be limited to the people within the particular agency or campus setting. There is a natural tendency to look first at what is best for ourselves as individuals and then for others close to us before we expand our view of the common good to a broader range of people. Our concept of community may be limited. We may consider the common good of only those within a particular agency, a campus locale, or a professional group. This conceptualization of community and this derivation of the common good may be sufficient for many ethical dilemmas, especially if the dilemmas are immediate crises. However, they are insufficient if staff want actively to help others, not just to avoid harming them. If student services is to create an ethical community, student services professionals need a community perspective that is broader than our immediate physical or professional communities.

Three community perspectives must be considered when establishing an ethical agenda for student servies: the earth as community, the United States as community, and higher education as community. Each community merits extensive consideration as individuals set forth agendas and establish priorities. This chapter illustrates how each of these community perspectives can affect the task of building an ethical agenda for student affairs. What is happening within these three communities that could affect everyone within them?

Earth as a Community. The threat of a nuclear holocaust has steadily increased since the bombing of Hiroshima and Nagasaki forty years ago. Scientists use the metaphor of a minute hand approaching midnight to portray how the world moves closer to extinction. This threat must be kept in mind when we formulate an ethical agenda. A concern for peace must be at the top of any prioritized list of ethical concerns, and it must be operationalized in daily interactions with students and colleagues. How can student service professionals confront peace issues? How can students be encouraged to confront, explore, and resolve these issues in their lives? How adequate is our own behavior in modeling interest, concern, and action in recognition of the earth as a community and of ourselves as members of that community who are responsible for what happens?

The United States as a Community. The individualism and the materialistic philosophies prevalent within the United States, while not unethical themselves, do not foster a climate conducive to considerations of the common good when we must make decisions about how to spend time or use resources. Poverty and pollution are important concerns for members of the earth's community, but they can also serve as a backdrop when we consider the needs and concerns of the community that makes up the United States. Society's ability to respond to social issues continues to be outpaced by the progress made in organizational development and technology. Experts hope that technological advances will solve the social issues, but so far they have not. We cannot ignore the social issues when we plan an ethical agenda and set priorities.

Higher Education as a Community. Higher education is a business, and in many instances it is a big business, although its aspirations are noble. It becomes concerned about recruitment and retention when enrollments diminish, it restricts students' course choices and increases classes sizes to enhance efficiency, and it relishes media and alumni attention to the accomplishments of its athletic programs. College bulletins espouse concern for the whole student, while programs, policies, and procedures often restrict the focus to grade point averages and professional credentialing. Ensuring a well-rounded education for all students seldom takes top priority. Administrators profess concern for providing good academic advising and teaching, yet they often reward publishing and grant-getting behaviors more generously. This corporate approach to administration has confused, disillusioned, and embittered many faculty and shortchanged many students.

Open-door policies have too often become swinging doors as entrance to college has become possible for increasing numbers of students, but the accessibility of success remains limited. Institutions are sometimes reluctant to recognize their responsibility to assist students who need help to succeed once they have been admitted.

Creating an Ethical Community: A Checklist. The concepts of earth, the United States, and higher education as communities become more manageable if examined in a checklist format. The table on this page serves as an example of how such a checklist might be applied to a campus setting by student services professionals. Factors such as the scope and depth of current professional activities and how they affect the ethical climate of the institution, and the implications for policy formulation and programmatic changes may become clearer if reviewed in this format.

Table 1. Checklist for Creating an Ethical Community

This checklist illustrates how ethical concerns for professional practice in student affairs can be used to assess the scope and depth of current professional activities that affect the ethical climate of the institution and to formulate policies and programs for future implementation. Sample activities are listed under five topical headings: peace issues and caring relationships, careers as vocations, theory and research into practice, personal development for all, and humane learning environment. On the right half of the page are the headings *when, how, who, whom,* and *impact.* Indicate *when* you or your agency acted on each item; *how* that intervention occurred; *who* or what agency was responsible; for *whom* the program, service, or intervention was intended; and what *impact* the program had as indicated by an evaluation. The checklist is intended to be a starting place for creation for your own checklist. Items can be added or changed to make the checklist more applicable to the individual setting.

Example:

Topic	When	How	Who	Whom	Impact
Humane learning environment Program to sensitize faculty to grading and testing issues.	First semester	Sponsored a day devoted to issues in classes, campus newspapers, panels.	Faculty, students	Faculty	50 percent faculty discussed in class, 35 percent reported change in practice

Topics and Program Examples

Peace issues and caring relationships
- International and national issues related to peace (examples: programs on arms race, effects of nuclear war)
- Cross-cultural awareness and understanding (examples: model United Nations, international student programs)
- Multicultural awareness and issues (examples: black history week, Chicano awareness programs, women's issues)
- Interpersonal relationships (examples: couple abuse, child and parent abuse, conflict resolution)

Careers as vocations for staff and faculty:
- Service role of professionals (example: meetings and workshops on service roles and conflicts)
- Stress and burnout among helpers (examples: time management and stress management programs)

For students:
- Integration of vocation concept into career-planning programs and career counseling (examples: dealing with values, life planning in career-planning programs)
- Volunteer and service options (example: volunteer programs for credit)

Theory and research into practice
- Improving knowledge base (examples: formal courses, informal seminars, brown baggers)
- Relationship of theory to practice (example: workshops devoted to developing theory-based practice)
- Contributions to knowledge base (example: participation in research and evaluation projects)
- Research implications for practice (example: using survey and other research to design intervention programs)

Personal development for all
- Needs assessment (example: obtaining needs assessment data from students and from developmental experts)
- Knowledge of services (example: targeted advertising programs)
- Developmental goals and advising (examples: integrating developmental advising)
- Development and the curriculum (examples: workshops on developmental theory and instruction, modules on developmental and ethical issues for course use)
- Institutional goals and human development (example: informal discussions on college goals)

Humane learning environment
- Recruitment (example: ensuring that students recruited have a fair chance of success)
- Retention (example: mentoring program for failing students, learning centers for learning-disabled students)
- Sensitization to student concerns (examples: programs and newsletters on test anxiety, causes and signs of suicide)

Implications for Planning an Ethical Agenda

The portrayals of the three communities in the preceding section were for the most part negative. They were not intended to be balanced or comprehensive but rather to suggest where the communities fall short of an ethical ideal. At the same time, they provide a structure for thinking about ethical issues and themes useful for planning an ethical agenda. This section explores five of the possible themes: peace issues, vocation as a calling, developmental progress for all students, theory and research as influences on professional practice, and a humane learning environment. What agenda items do these themes suggest?

Peace Issues. Concern for peace calls for ethical action in three spheres of professional and personal life: responses to national and international issues related to peace and war; recognition of the oneness of the campus community as it is reflected in interactions between offices, agencies, staff and students, and staff and faculty; and responding to others as members of the human community.

Issues related to peace are much broader than disarmament and war. A task analysis of what it would take to arrive at peace could result in a series of enabling tasks or steps that would lead to peace as the final objective. However, peace is not possible without an understanding of other nations and cultures in the world, of ethnic groups within our own country, and of our own neighbors. It is important for students to explore issues related to the arms race, disarmament, and conflict resolution at international levels. It is a hopeful sign that Congress has approved a Peace Academy. The emergence of peace majors on college campuses is another healthful sign. Student services staffs need to determine their roles in promoting and facilitating the development of peace majors, course units that explore peace issues and conflict resolution, and symposiums and programs using local and national speakers to address these critical issues. Many facets of student services relate directly and indirectly to promoting international understanding through the forums of student activities and the policies and programs for foreign students.

Conflicts within the campus community are perhaps not as visible now as they were a decade or two ago. Nevertheless, *how* student services interacts as an agency or as professionals with one another or with students and faculty provides a model that students can emulate. Failure to confront issues can be harmful. If students are aware of backsliding, staff are failing to provide examples of how confrontation can take place in a caring fashion. Student services professionals are in a unique teaching position; it is an opportunity that they cannot ignore.

Finally, peace on this planet is affected by how individuals react to one another. Professional roles may not often provide the opportunity to work toward peace through campus programming or to model caring confrontation through agency interactions, but there are daily one-to-one contacts with staff, faculty, and students. These opportunities can be used to demonstrate civility and courtesy, regardless of status. Perhaps there will never be world peace until individuals have removed the violence and hatred from within themselves. Efforts to reduce the subtle and covert violence in our own behavior are another essential step toward peace.

Vocation as a Calling. Winston and Dagley suggest in Chapter Four that one characteristic of a profession is that its members have a sense that they have a "calling." This is an important theme for an ethical agenda for professionals in student services and for work in career planning with students. The calling for student services professionals probably comes later in their career development than it does for others. Few high school students picture their future as being dean of students, director of a residence hall, or college counselor. They more often enter the profession by accident than by design. Involvement comes about through the combination of skills and interests in the right place at the right time. Many people have entered student services because they work well with students, which often is a reflection of an honest caring for students as well as of talent. It is important to recognize and maintain this motivation through periods of burnout and insufficient reinforcement. It is important not to lose sight of one primary motivation, serving others.

Career counseling was one of the first service roles for student personnel staff in higher education, and it remains an essential and much-used service. American society and many students define career success as status and material gains. The need to help others is given too few opportunities for fulfillment. It is important in career planning to help students to become aware of the strength of this need, of the importance that it may come to have in the future, and of how it might be possible to match current needs with expected needs in making career plans. A study of the student's values should be an integral part of career planning.

Developmental Progress for All. Opportunities to master mathematics, writing, or even recreational skills are available to most students. The student enrolls in related courses, receives instruction, and avails himself or herself of numerous campus resources in order to master the content. At most institutions, students are required to take certain courses related to institutional goals. Academic achievement is accessible to all within parameters limited by their abilities and institutional resources. It is accessible not only because the resources are available but also because the institution demonstrates its commitment by requiring courses or demonstrated competence and by assessing and recording progress.

The same is not true for developmental goals. Perhaps in theory every student could be said to have the opportunity to enhance his or her career development, leadership skills, life-planning skills, interpersonal skills, or awareness of his or her value system. For the most part, however, opportunities to pursue personal developmental goals are neither structured nor required, and achievements are seldom assessed or recorded. It is not sufficient to say that the opportunities are present when there is no formal system for full student participation and no value assigned (for example, in the form of credit). Academic accomplishments are fostered directly and intentionally. Personal development goals are supported only indirectly through optional programs and services, and students' accomplishments in this domain are often accidental rather than intentional.

Student services and student development educators can work to make developmental goals truly accessible to more (if not all) students by working directly with students and by working with the system. Examples of direct approaches to students include initiating systematic needs assessments that embrace developmental theory as well as examine student wants. Designing and implementing programs to meet these needs is the next important step. Advertising programs is also critical. One index of true accessibility is when commuter as well as on-campus students use the programs and opportunities thus provided. Such use is an indication that students are aware of the developmental opportunities and that they value them. Mentoring and student development transcript systems (Brown and DeCoster, 1982) are other ways of demonstrating that the system values developmental accomplishments and that these accomplishments can be documented for student use.

Indirect approaches to making developmental opportunities available to all students include working with the system whenever opportunities can be created or used to weave developmental goals into the fabric of the academic program. The possibilities for integrating academic and personal development have not been exhausted. Developmental theory has been used to assist college instructors to understand how students process and react to ideas and instructional strategies. Student services staff should cherish opportunities to work with professors to help them understand how students think about ideas, but they must also help professors to realize that understanding how students feel and think about themselves and other people is also important.

Student services staffs and developmental educators could develop instructional modules that integrated course content with developmental goals. They could determine what subject matter areas were most adaptable, and they could identify individual faculty who were most receptive to using the modules. Joint grant-seeking efforts by faculty and staff to obtain funding for module development would be an ideal approach to developing faculty-staff partnerships. Each year, different departments could be targeted or adopted for an intensive campaign of work with faculty. The possibility that these same faculty could provide beneficial counsel to students affairs should not be ignored.

Theory and Research. A physician is expected to know the latest developments in medicine and to be able to apply them to his or her practice. Similar expectations hold for the lawyer and other professionals. The same must be true for student services professionals. The advances in theory and applied research of the past twenty years provide an understanding of how students develop in college and of the programs and kinds of environments that facilitate development and retention. This body of knowledge is no longer speculative or theoretical. Neither young nor old professionals have an excuse for not being aware of this knowledge or for not applying it in their practice. Senior student services officers are not being ethically responsible if they proceed as if this rich source of literature did not exist or as if it were not relevant. Budgets must be in the black, and programs and services must be administered efficiently, but the central purpose of the programs and services must not be lost in efforts to be efficient. Accountability requires more than simple efficiency.

Researchers in student services and those pursuing research on developmental issues need to align themselves with program developers and program evaluators to assess the effectiveness of programs and environments that facilitate student development and provide a humane learning environment. Researchers who conduct surveys on student behavior or attitudes should also feel compelled to follow up on their surveys with research evaluation projects that use survey results to assess the impact of intervention programs. Surveys are needed for planning and comparisons, but it is irresponsible for researchers to continue to conduct surveys on alcohol use, depression on campus, or developmental levels of various student groups without subsequent follow-up efforts that result in programs and evaluations.

A Humane Learning Environment. Higher education is unlike almost any other environment imaginable. Ideally, it should be stimulating, challenging, and rewarding as an intellectual and personal development experience. For many students it is. But, the college environment can also be perceived as hostile. It can be threatening, unrewarding, and a negative experience for many students. It is easy to forget the 50 percent who withdraw from college; not all are academic failures. There are numbers of students whose future associations to their college experience will emphasize missed opportunities, boredom, and sadness.

Student services professionals must not forget the rising tide of suicide among college-age youth. The suicide rate among fifteen- to twenty-four-year-olds has tripled since the 1950s, and young adults between the ages of twenty and twenty-four have had nearly twice the rate of suicides as teenagers fifteen to nineteen years old (Rosenberg and others, 1984; Mercy and others, 1984). Student failures are not due to the system alone, nor are suicides among young adults caused solely by the college environment, but it is important to be reminded that collegiate life is not necessarily a sanctuary from life's woes; it may in fact accentuate them.

Student services can help to provide a humane learning environment by maintaining an academic safety net for students. Admissions and recruiting policies and programs need to be scrutinized for their forthrightness in advising students who do not have the skills necessary to succeed in college. Advising and remedial programs must be provided for students who have weaknesses that could mean failure early in their academic career. Test-anxiety programs and career planning to help students match ability and interests to career plans are appropriate responses to the sometimes unfriendly academic environment. Doing everything possible to assist capable and interested students succeed in college is an ethical responsibility. A sink or swim philosophy is not a responsible ethical posture for public higher education. It is for that reason that we opened our editor's notes with the case of the less than compassionate student dean.

A systems approach to providing a humane learning environment is another ethical responsibility. Applying Band-Aids to the wounded is not sufficient. Student services must do its best to make the system responsive to students. This means a fair admissions program, a diagnostic approach to student academic proficiencies, equitable financial aid programs, provisions for students with academic skill deficiencies, grading systems that are forthright and based on valid assessments, realistic graduation requirements, and student-focused placement activities. Student affairs professionals have the opportunity and the obligation to work with students and faculty to make the learning environment more humane.

Closing Comments

Higher education is in great need of a new way of thinking and acting on ethical principles. This will require a shift in customary styles and work habits that may transform professional lives and higher education in radical ways. It may be empirically untested, but a good working hypothesis is that optimal student development is most likely to occur in an ethical climate (Canon, 1983). If this assumption is true, professionals must work to improve the ethical climate on their campuses. Creating an ethical climate on campus is both an essential and a possible mission for student services.

Taking positions on ethical issues is not easy, whether it involves confronting a colleague, a faculty member, or an administrator. At the extreme, it can mean ostracism and loss of a job. Constant questioning can mean loss of credibility. Nevertheless, if student affairs professionals are persistent, patient, and prudent, they stand a chance of being recognized for honest and caring concern that merits attention and response.

This sourcebook serves its purpose if it heightens the reader's awareness of ethical issues on campus, but there are many other potential uses as well. The checklist allows the reader to determine how active he or she and his or her staff and campus are in creating an ethical climate on campus. The ethical codes in the Appendixes are handy resources. The case studies described by Canon in Chapter One, the principles provided by Kitchener in Chapter Two, and the matrix schema presented by Krager in Chapter Three could serve as discussion items for staff meetings. The theme of this chapter and of the rest of the book is that we must be active in developing an ethical agenda and that such an agenda should lead to action as well as to reaction.

References

Bowen, H. R. *The State of the Nation and the Agenda for Higher Education.* San Francisco: Jossey-Bass, 1982.

Brown, R. D., and DeCoster, D. A. (Eds.). *Mentoring-Transcript Systems for Promoting*

Student Growth. New Directions in Student Services, no. 19. San Francisco: Jossey-Bass, 1982.

Canon, H. J. "The Ethical Climate and Student Development." Paper presented at the American College Personnal Association annual meeting, Houston, March 15, 1983.

Mercy, J. A., Tolsma, D. D., Smith, J. C., and Conn, J. M. "Patterns of Youth Suicide in the United States." *Educational Horizons,* 1984, *62* (4), 124–127.

Rosenberg, M. L., Mercy, J. A., and Smith, J. C. "Violence as a Public Health Problem: A New Role for CDC and a New Alliance with Educators." *Educational Horizons,* 1984, *62* (4), 124–127.

Robert D. Brown is professor of educational psychology and measurements at the University of Nebraska-Lincoln. The editor of the Journal of College Student Personnel, *he is the recipient of the American College Personnel Association's Contribution to Knowledge Award.*

Commonly held beliefs about ethics are examined, and the potential of an ethics of care is described.

How to Think About Professional Ethics

*Harry J. Canon
Robert D. Brown*

The preceding chapters make it clear that the pursuit of ethical truths and the sustaining of ethical behaviors are intellectually demanding tasks. These efforts are also emotionally demanding; they require high levels of personal courage and a substantial measure of persistence. Thinking about ethics can be intimidating. This concluding chapter enumerates and challenges some of the prevalent myths that inhibit clear thinking about professional ethics, and it closes with an exploration of the relationship between the process of caring and our thinking about ethics. If student services professionals can discard common notions about ethics and substitute an ethics of care as the motivating core, then ethical thinking will be a natural, expected activity and thus have a profound impact on daily professional practice.

Ethical Myths

Myths often serve as convenient explanations for behavior. They provide a rationale for taking action or, perhaps more often in the case of ethical myths, for avoiding action. Some of the more common myths about ethics follow with brief commentary and challenge.

Personal ethical perfection (or near perfection) is prerequisite to any serious ethical inquiry. The Methodist minister father of one of the authors occasionally encountered people who declined to attend worship services on the grounds that those who went to church were mostly hypocrites who failed to follow the teachings of the Scriptures. His usual response was to observe that the church was created for sinners; those who had already achieved perfection probably had no need for such an institution.

That observation appears to be capable of valid translation into the secular goal of enhancing standards of ethical conduct. Everyone is, if you will, a sinner in so far as each of us falls short of any ultimate ethical ideal. Kitchener, Krager, and Winston and Dagley have already spoken to the difficulties in identifying ultimate ethical truths. It is therefore also reasonable to accept personal ethical lapses and shortcomings as part of being human. Pursuit of professional ethical concerns does not reflect self-righteous posturing but rather serves to acknowledge personal fallibility and a desire to achieve a higher level of ethical functioning.

Ethics are just value judgments, and one person's values are as good as another's. Kitchener noted that no reasonable person would accord parity to the value decisions of an Adolf Hitler and of a Martin Luther King. In fact, the issue is even more complex than that.

Institutions of higher education share a rich and absolutely essential system of values. Within that system, values are arranged in a hierarchical order. Because the discovery of truth has primacy, provisions for free inquiry and an open forum are absolutely essential. In adhering to the principle of maintaining an open forum, colleges and universities commonly tolerate expressions that would be considered outrageous in any other setting, expressions that may be offensive to certain members of the campus community and demeaning of their personal dignity. At the same time, the academic community also places a high value on the worth and dignity of the individual. Where the values of the open forum and the dignity of the individual come into conflict, the importance of the open forum is held paramount. At the same time, the transcendent value assigned to the open forum also assures opportunity for rebuttal and increases the likelihood that attacks on persons will be labeled for what they are—inappropriate to serious intellectual discourse and beneath the dignity of thoughtful persons. The institutions that we serve and our professional commitments require adherence to these and other transcendent ethical values. Some values are better than others.

It's my First Amendment right! Sure it is. But there is usually a price to pay in the exercise of one's First Amendment rights, and that price may be more than the individual or other members of the community can afford.

This assertion is an inevitable component in any dispute with the student press, and it may crop up as staff members and colleagues express the desire to give wider circulation to a concern of the moment. Most professionals are inclined to beat a quick retreat in the face of any suggestion that they are interfering with First Amendment rights. On some occasions, a thoughtful examination of the specific issues raised by the matter at hand might lead to other courses of action. It might be useful, for example, to consider the consequences of making certain events, facts, or conjectures public. Do rumors that are potentially damaging to community members and that are not for attribution warrant publication? Is it in the best interests of higher education to make the details of performance evaluations of senior administrators a matter of public record? What are the consequences for their ability to lead? Do ad hominem attacks qualify for legitimate First Amendment protection? Is the racist or sexist cartoon on the editorial page immune from challenge? And, how do professionals deal with the fact that neither next-day retractions nor subsequent letters to the editor adequately compensate for the damage done by partial truths or even by well-intentioned but professionally marginal journalism? There is a valid and critical difference between sloganeering and legitimate assertion of a constitutional right. Student services professionals have an ethical responsibility to be certain that they do not suspend their intellectual and critical faculties when confronted with otherwise valid ethical or constitutional phraseology that has (perhaps in good faith) been converted into sloganeering.

Value clarification workshops are the answer if we want to improve professional ethical practices. This claim is probably not true. We surely need to be clear on what our values are, but if they fall short of necessary professional standards, we still have a problem.

The observations made in preceding paragraphs apply here as well: Some values are better than others. The student services professions and academe require allegiance to some ordered values. What is really needed is to be clear about those values and to be consistent in pursuing them.

The answers to ethical dilemmas lie in our ethical code. Codes are helpful, but they cannot address or anticipate every conceivable real-life dilemma, as Winston and Dagley amply demonstrate in Chapter Four.

Dealing with ethical violations is the job of our ethics committee. Referring all problems directly to an association's ethics committee is the rough equivalent of calling a cop to deal with a neighbor's loud stereo. It may eventually come to that if the difficulty is to be resolved, but responsible adult behavior and responsible professional behavior require that we first directly contact the offending (or potentially offending) individual. One begins with the assumption — usually accurate — that the offending party does not intend to offend. If that turns out to be so, the matter is quickly resolved as a consequence of directing the offender's attention to the questionable behavior. Reversing the circumstances may help to make the point. If and when it becomes necessary to challenge us on the ethical quality of some aspect of our professional behavior, we would prefer being approached informally by a colleague whose office is down the hall than receiving a letter from the chair of the ACPA ethics committee. It might not be pleasant to experience the former; but it would be devastating to encounter the formality of the latter. Further, there is always the possibility that the observer of the alleged infraction has failed to appreciate the particular circumstances or that he or she has simply erred; the personal contact might help to prevent an escalation that could eventually be an embarrassment to all parties involved. The necessary conclusion is that we should call the cop (or our ethics committee) only after our own attempt to address the matter has proved ineffective.

People are either ethical, or they are not. It is as simple as that. This claim is not very likely to be true. Even the best tend to become inadvertently self-serving if left wholly to their own devices. Conversely—Brown speaks to this point in Chapter Five—to the extent that we are surrounded by caring friends who share our concern for high ethical standards, we increase the chances that our attention will be directed to those instances when we fall short.

A thoughtful and conscientious professional knows when he or she commits an ethical violation. This claim is not necessarily so. Refer to the preceding paragraph, which highlights the tendency to be self-serving. Quite beyond that, ethical decision making is so complex that no one of us acting alone is likely to envision all the ethical implications of a particular aspect of our behavior. We need a little help from our friends.

Ethics are all very fine, but one also has to be practical. Being ethical is itself a very practical pursuit. Individuals, enterprises, and institutions that place a high premium on respecting autonomy, avoiding the doing of harm, benefiting others, being just, and being faithful establish a degree of credibility with others that tends to earn loyalty, trust, and respect in return. Individuals are ultimately dependent on the responses of others—both friends and adversaries—for whatever measure of success they might hope to enjoy in their personal and professional endeavors. Behavior that is consistent with the principles enunciated by Kitchener in Chapter Two may lose the occasional battle; its very predictability increases the odds of winning the war.

If people would just follow the ethical codes of their professions, life would be a lot less complicated. This statement is both true and false. Professional lives would probably be somewhat less complicated. But, there are also two problems with this myth. First, all the student services ethical codes put together still add up to a lower operational standard than most professionals are willing to accept. Second, it is unlikely that there would be consistent agreement on what a given provision of a given code means in daily practice.

Winston and Dagley described in Chapter Four how the ethical codes of the several student services professional organizations differ and how those differences might produce bias that favors one constituency over another. Those biases in themselves suggest a less than optimal level of ethical functioning. There is another limitation. Codes commonly represent principles on which a large number of persons can agree. The requirement for such agreement inevitably results in a watering down process that results in a series of statements that represent only the minimum standards. If the members of a given professional association were polled on the question, Does your ethical code adequately cover the ethical issues that you consider to be important to your professional practice? it is likely that the majority would answer no. The compromises that are essential to the democratic process of developing and adopting a code also serve to produce a less stringent and less demanding document.

The likelihood of an agreed-upon, consensual interpretation of a specific ethical code provision tends to decrease when specific and immediate decisions are involved. Real-life situations engage emotions, cause people to take sides, commonly result in defensive behavior, and otherwise lead to the taking of polarized positions. Few issues strike closer to home for the professional than the implication that he or she has been even moderately deficient in adhering to professional ethical standards. Thus, a consensual interpretation of a code provision becomes difficult to obtain.

Ultimately, trying to be ethical winds up as an incredibly intense personal journey. As Winston and Dagley observe in Chapter Four, professional codes are quite helpful, but they are scarcely the ultimate solution. Krager's charts and Kitchener's principles advance our thinking, but they still leave us short of ethical perfection. Certainly, none of the four pretends to do more than offer external guidelines for a lifelong journey that may be shared with an external community (as Brown argues in Chapter Five) but that also involves paths where each of us is necessarily alone. The occasional loneliness and uncertainty can be somewhat mitigated if we are consistent in our reexamination of common beliefs and assumptions, such as those outlined earlier in this section. Demythologizing is a necessary and honorable part of the search for ethical truths.

An Ethics of Care

Until quite recently, the study of ethics has been considered to be complex, logical, and abstract. To think clearly about ethical issues, a person had to be legalistic and highly rational. Logical thinking and ethical inquiry were viewed as being synonymous. Emotions and the affective domain were excluded from ethical thought. Thinking and reasoning were viewed as more germane than feeling. Although this perspective was not universal among ethicists, it is safe to say that it has been the dominant paradigm for thinking about ethics.

More recently, increased attention is being given to other ways of thinking about ethics. Research and careful analyses of feminine approaches to ethical thinking prompt considerations of new ways to conceptualize ethical decision making. Women do not respond to ethical and moral dilemmas as men do, and the implications of these findings for our thinking about ethics are now being explored.

Gilligan (1982) is prominent among the developmental researchers who suggest that the feminine perspective is important in examinations of ethical issues. She reports that the masculine approach to ethics emphasizes the protection of individual rights and the promulgation of general rules. It is regulations and codes that are important in the masculine scheme. Women, in general, are more likely than men to be concerned with the human relationships involved in ethical dilemmas, and they are also more likely to search for a resolution that fits the specific context rather than to seek to propose a general rule. A feminine perspective on ethics is not lower than the masculine perspective, but it is different, and this difference has important implications for thinking about professional ethics. Gilligan suggests an ethics of care. This ethics of care would be concerned more with relationships than with rules and more with the context of the particular dilemmas than with universal laws.

Noddings (1984) also proposes an ethics of care and suggests that it does not imply a rejection of the cognitive or of rational thinking. Rationality is still valued, but in her view it must serve something higher. That something higher is a caring for others. Her work illustrates the implications of an ethics of care for many everyday situations that call for ethical decisions. She also suggests numerous implications for educational systems as well. Noddings goes so far as to suggest that the primary aim of education must be the maintenance and enhancement of caring. In Noddings's eyes, an ethics based on caring influences instructor and student roles and other relationships that affect instructional practices and student evaluations.

Delworth and Seeman (1984) suggest several implications of an ethics of care for student services professionals. They note that this perspective could affect how career counselors relate to women clients, who place relationships above competition. They also suggest how an institution could examine its policies to determine how an ethics of care might be implemented.

An ethics of care is not foreign to student services professionals but rather is highly congruent with the mission of the profession and with the values of those attracted to the profession. The profession is premised on the need for caring for individual students and on the need for supporting those who are reasonably effective in establishing close and meaningful relationships with students. It may be an oversimplification, but professors are often concerned both about their subject matter and about students; student services professionals are concerned primarily about students, although they undoubtedly have other distracting or conflicting allegiances.

However, student services professionals are seldom fully comfortable with their student-centered focus. There is a prevailing perception that many faculty and administrators see a student-centered focus as "soft," perhaps even as "mindless." Administrators are perceived to believe that it is appropriate to have the best interests of students in mind but concurrently to hold the belief that decisions must be based on the promulgated rules and regulations of the institution rather than on the needs of individual students. Some of the myths described earlier relate to this kind of thinking. Thus, because student services professionals tend to put individual student concerns above general regulations or because they tend to think emotionally about issues, they tend also to perceive themselves as being less intellectual and less rational.

There is not enough space to fully present the ethics of care. It is also too early to say where this new line of thought about moral and ethical reasoning will lead. Clearly, more research and thought are needed. However, we would be remiss not to provide this perspective in a sourcebook on ethics for the student services professions. The importance of an ethics of care lies in its potential for providing a framework for student services professionals that allows them to think about their professional roles. It is a perspective that fits their natural interests in caring for others and in being cared for, it bolsters job descriptions in the appropriate direction, and it may well both provide principles for and justify ethical decisions that they make. The importance of relationships and of thinking contextually, two cornerstones of ethical care, are a natural fit with student development goals and the student services profession.

References

Delworth, U., and Seeman, D. "The Ethics of Care: Implications of Gilligan for the Student Services Profession." *Journal of College Student Personnel,* 1984, *25* (6), 489–492.
Gilligan, C. *In a Different Voice.* Cambridge, Mass.: Harvard University Press, 1982.
Noddings, N. *Caring: A Feminine Approach to Ethics and Moral Education.* Berkeley, Calif.: University of California Press, 1984.

Harry J. Canon is professor of leadership and educational policy studies at Northern Illinois University and current chair of the Professional Ethics and Conduct Committee of the American College Personnel Association.

Robert D. Brown is professor of educational psychology and measurements at the University of Nebraska–Lincoln. The editor of the Journal of College Student Personnel, *he is the recipient of the American College Personnel Association's Contribution to Knowledge Award.*

Appendixes

APPENDIX 1.
American College Personnel Association Statement of Ethical and Professional Standards

Preamble

The American College Personnel Association, a division of the American Association of Counseling and development, is an educational, scientific, and professional organization whose members are dedicated to enhancing the worth, dignity, potential, and uniqueness of each individual and thus to the service of society. Although members work in various postsecondary educational settings, they are committed to protecting individual human rights, advancing knowledge of college student growth and development, and promoting effectiveness in student affairs organizations and operations. As a means of supporting these commitments, members of the American College Personnel Association subscribe to the following standards of ethical and professional conduct.

These standards are designed to provide a guide for ethical and professional behavior in general student affairs practice and to complement the existing Ethical Standards of the American Association of Counseling and Development. Members in specialized student affairs settings are also encouraged to consult ethical standards specific to their settings.

A. Relationships With Students

1. Members treat students as individuals who possess dignity, worth, and the ability to be self-directed and assist students in becoming productive, responsible citizens and members of society. Members are concerned for the welfare of all students and work for constructive change on behalf of students.

2. Members respect the student's right of self-determination. The student's freedom of choice should be limited only when the individual's decisions or actions may result in significant damage to self, to others, or to the institution.

3. Members explicitly inform students of the nature and/or limits of confidentiality in noncounseling as well as in counseling relationships.

4. Members respect the student's right to privacy and share information about individuals only in accordance with institutional policies, or when given permission by the student, or when required to prevent personal harm.

5. Members confront students in a professional manner with issues and behaviors that have ethical implications.

B. General Responsibilities

1. Members contribute to the development of the profession through sharing skills and program ideas, serving professional organizations, educating emerging professionals, improving professional practices, keeping abreast of contemporary theories and applications, and conducting and reporting research.

2. Members realize professional growth is continuous and cumulative and is characterized by a well-defined philosophy that explains why and how members function in the student affairs profession. Members base this philosophy upon sound theoretical principles and an explicitly examined personal value system (assuming congruence with the basic assumptions from the student personnel point of view and the student development point of view).

3. Members model ethically responsible behavior for students and colleagues and expect ethical behavior among members and nonmembers at all times. When

information is possessed which raises serious doubt as to the ethical behavior of professional colleagues, whether Association members or not, members are encouraged to take action to rectify such a condition. Possible actions include (a) confronting the individual in question, (b) utilizing institutional channels, and/or (c) using available Association mechanisms.

   4. Members do not seek self-enhancement or self-aggrandizement through evaluations or comparisons that are damaging to others.

   5. Members perform in a fashion that is not discriminatory on the basis of race, sex, national origin, affectional/sexual preference, handicap, age, or creed, and they work actively to modify discriminatory practices when encountered.

   6. Members maintain and enhance professional effectiveness by improving skills and acquiring new knowledge through systematic continuing education and assure the same opportunity for persons under their supervision.

   7. Members monitor their personal functioning and effectiveness and when needed seek assistance from appropriate professionals (for example, colleague, physician, counselor, attorney).

   8. Members accurately represent their professional credentials, competencies, and limitations to all concerned and are responsible for correcting any misrepresentations of these qualifications by others.

   9. Members have a clear responsibility to ensure that information provided to the public or subordinates, peers, and supervisors is factual, accurate, and unbiased.

   10. Members establish fees for professional services after consideration of fees charged by other professionals delivering comparable services and the ability of the recipient to pay. Members provide some services for which they receive little or no remuneration.

   11. Members demonstrate sensible regard for the social codes and moral expectations of the communities in which they live and work. They recognize that violations of accepted moral and legal standards may involve their clients, students, or colleagues in damaging personal conflicts and may impugn their own reputations, the integrity of the profession, and the reputation of the employing institution.

   12. Members maintain ethical relationships with colleagues and students and refrain from relationships which impinge on the dignity, moral code, self-worth, professional functioning, and/or personal growth of these individuals. Specifically, members are aware that sexual relationships hold great potential for exploitation. Consequently, members refrain from having sexual relationships with anyone to whom they act as counselors or therapists. Sexual relationships with staff members or students for whom one has supervisory or evaluative responsibilities have high potential for causing personal damage and for limiting the exercise of professional responsibilities and are therefore unprofessional and unethical.

C. Professional and Collegial Relationships

   1. Members seek to collaborate and to share expertise with other student affairs staff members, faculty members, administrators, and students.

   2. Members contribute periodically to the professional development of colleagues with no compensation other than for immediate expenses.

   3. Members accurately acknowledge contributions to program development, program implementation, evaluations, and reports made by others.

   4. Members support the appropriate efforts of fellow student affairs professionals and institutional programs. Constructive criticism and professional disagreements are shared (in private when possible) with those individuals concerned and in a manner that is not demeaning.

   5. Members establish working agreements with subordinates and supervisors

that clearly define accountability procedures, mutual expectations, evaluation criteria, position duties, and decision-making procedures.

6. Members conduct themselves in such a manner that their positions are not used to seek unjustified personal gains, sexual favors, or unfair advantages, including goods and services not normally accorded those in such positions.

7. Members regularly evaluate the professional development and job performance of direct line subordinate staff members and recommend appropriate actions to enhance professional development and improve job performance.

8. Members seek regular evaluations of their job performance and professional development from colleagues, supervisors, and clientele.

9. Members are fair and unbiased in judgments they render about persons with whom they work. Members have a right to expect that colleagues and supervisors will strive to render fair and unbiased judgments about them. Members respect the rights of others to differ in the judgments and evaluations they render so long as these judgments are not intended to do harm or disservice.

10. Members have the right to request and to receive support from the Association in matters of ethical practice and standards as defined herein.

D. Institutional Relationships

1. Members make contributions to their employing institution in support of its goals, missions, and policies.

2. Members ensure that accurate presentations of institutional goals, services, programs, and policies are made to the public students, prospective students, colleagues, and subordinates.

3. Members inform appropriate officials of conditions that may be potentially disruptive or damaging to the institution's mission, personnel, and property.

4. Members inform employers of conditions which may limit or curtail the members' effectiveness.

5. Members have responsibilities both to the individuals served and to the institution within which the service is performed. The acceptance of employment in an institution implies that members are in general agreement with the mission of the institution. Therefore, the professional activities of members are expected to be in accord with the mission of the institution.

6. When the member and the institution encounter substantial disagreements or conflicts concerning professional or personal values, the member has the responsibility to directly and constructively seek resolution of the conflicts. Resolution of such conflicts may result either in sustained efforts to modify institutional policies and practices or in a decision by the member to terminate the institutional affiliation.

7. Members regularly and systematically evaluate those programs, services, and courses for which they are responsible in accord with sound evaluation principles and make these evaluation results available to appropriate institutional personnel.

E. Employment and Hiring Practices

1. Employers widely disseminate advertisements and notices which accurately and clearly describe: (a) responsibilities of the position; (b) information about the institution; (c) necessary qualifications, such as education, skills, and experiences; (d) salary range and benefits; (e) special restrictions, if any (for example, live-in requirements, night work expectations, travel requirements, positions of a temporary nature).

2. Employers clearly specify in writing the interview and selection process to the applicant and strictly follow that process. Applicants are periodically notified of the status of their applications during the selection process.

3. Employers do not discriminate against applicants on the basis of race, color, creed, sex, national origin, affectional/sexual preference, age, or handicap.

4. Employers hire only individuals for professional positions who have received educational preparation experiences appropriate for the requirements of the positions.

5. Employers provide opportunities during the interviewing process for the applicant to gain accurate information about institutional colleagues, policies, philosophy, and about position requirements and responsibilities.

6. Employers notify employees within a minimum of thirty days when terminating or changing the status of their employment, specifying reasons and providing full due process rights.

7. Applicants accurately represent their education, skills, and experiences.

8. Applicants respond to job offers without undue delay. Applicants accept only those professional positions they intend to assume. Both applicants and employers honor mutually derived contracts.

9. Applicants advise all institutions at which applications are pending immediately when they have signed a contract and are withdrawing from the applicant pool.

10. Members inform their employers a minimum of thirty days before leaving their positions.

F. Research, Publication, and Written Communication

1. Members are aware of and responsive to all pertinent ethical principles when planning any research activity dealing with human subjects (see *Ethical Principles in the Conduct of Research with Human Participants,* Washington, D.C.: American Psychological Association, 1973).

2. Members who serve as principal researchers are ultimately responsible for assuring that all research activities conform to ethical standards. Others involved in the research activities share full and equal responsibility.

3. Members are responsible for the welfare of their research subjects throughout the study and take precautions to prevent injurious psychological, physical, or social effects:
   a. When control groups are used, care is exercised to assure that they are not deprived of services to which they are entitled.
   b. When withholding information or providing misinformation to subjects is essential to the investigation (provided the conditions above are met), members fully inform subjects about the nature of the research and take corrective action as soon as possible following data collection.
   c. Participation in research is expected to be voluntary.

4. Members disguise the identity of the subjects when supplying data or when reporting research results unless specific authorization to do otherwise has been given by such subjects.

5. Members conduct and report investigations in a manner that minimizes the possibility that results will be misleading.

6. Members become familar with and give recognition to previous work on the topic (both published and unpublished), observe all copyright laws, and give full credit to all to whom credit is due when conducting and reporting research.

7. Members who agree to cooperate with another individual in research and/or publication must cooperate as promised in terms of punctuality of performance and with equal regard for the completeness and accuracy of the information provided.

8. Members acknowledge major contributions to research projects and professional writings through joint authorships, listing the author who made the principal contribution first. Minor contributions of a professional or technical nature are acknowledged in footnotes or introductory statements.

9. Members do not demand coauthorship of publications when their involvement has been ancillary. Teachers and/or supervisors exercise caution when working with students and/or subordinate staff so as not to unduly pressure them for joint authorship.

10. Members make sufficient original research data available to qualified others who may wish to replicate the study.

11. Members communicate to other professionals the results of any research judged to be of professional or scientific value. Results reflecting unfavorably on specific institutions, programs, services, or vested interests should not be withheld for such reasons.

12. Members submit manuscripts to only one journal when seeking publication of an article. If not accepted by that journal the manuscript may then be submitted to another journal. Members do not seek publication of the same material in more than one publication without receiving consent from the editors and/or publishers involved. Slightly altered, previously published manuscripts or manuscripts under review are not submitted without first informing the editors of both publications.

G. Professional Preparation and Development

Members who are responsible for teaching others should be guided by statements on professional preparation issued by the Association and relevant accrediting agencies. Members who function as faculty members assume unique ethical responsibilities that frequently go beyond that of members who do not function in this capacity.

1. Members inform prospective students of program expectations, basic skills needed for successful completion, and employment prospects prior to admission to the program. Information about programs based on a particular theoretical position is clearly communicated to students upon application.

2. Members ensure that experiences focusing on self-understanding or growth are voluntary or, if required as part of the program, are made known to prospective students prior to entering the program. When the program offers a growth experience with an emphasis on self-disclosure or other relatively intimate or personal involvement, members should have no administrative, supervisory, or evaluative authority regarding the participant.

3. Members support preparation program efforts by providing practicum settings, field placements, and consultation to students and/or faculty members.

4. Members in charge of preparation programs ensure that such programs integrate both academic study and supervised practice.

5. Members develop and implement clear policies within their institution regarding field placement and the roles of the student and the supervisor in such placements.

6. Members present thoroughly varied theoretical positions or make provision for their study so that students may develop a broad base of knowledge.

7. Members establish programs directed toward developing students' skills, knowledge, and self-understanding, stated whenever possible in terms of competency or performance.

8. Members identify the level of competence of the student during and at the end of the programs and communicate these assessments to the student.

9. Members, through continual student evaluation and appraisal, are aware of any personal limitations of the students that might impede future performance. Members not only assist students in securing remedial assistance but also screen from the program those students who are judged unable to perform as a competent professional.

10. Members provide programs that include research components commensurate

with the levels of expected functioning. Paraprofessional and technician-level personnel should be trained as consumers of research and should learn how to evaluate their own and their program's effectiveness. Advanced graduate education, especially at the doctoral level, includes preparation for conducting original research.

11. Members make students aware of the ethical responsibilities and standards of the profession by distributing and discussing this document and other relevant documents.

12. Members conduct professional preparation in keeping with the most current guidelines of American Association of Counseling and Development and the American College Personnel Association.

13. Members who serve as preparation program faculty members and/or practitioners aid in providing in-service development programs and educational experiences to one another.

H. Counseling and Testing

This section constitutes general guidelines for counseling and testing experiences frequently encountered by student affairs professionals. Those professionals who are engaged in intensive counseling and/or testing activities are urged to consult the American Association of Counseling and Development's Ethical Standards for more specific standards.

To the extent that the student's choice of action is not imminently self- or other destructive, the student must retain freedom of choice.

1. The counseling relationship and information resulting therefrom must be kept confidential, consistent with the obligations of the member as a professional person.

2. Members who learn from counseling relationships of conditions that are likely to harm the client or others immediately report the condition to a responsible authority in order to preclude harm.

3. Members inform students of the conditions and/or limitations under which they may receive counseling assistance or before the time when the counseling relationship is entered. This is particularly so when conditions exist of which the student could be unaware.

4. Records of the counseling relationship, including interview notes, test data, correspondence, tape recordings, and other documents, are to be considered professional information for use in counseling, and they are not part of the public or official records of the institution or agency in which the counselor is employed. Revelation to others of counseling records shall occur only upon the expressed consent of the client or upon court order.

5. Members avoid initiating a counseling relationship or terminate an existing relationship if they are unable to be of professional assistance to the student. In either event, members refer the student to an appropriate specialist. (Members must be knowledgeable about referral resources so that a satisfactory referral can be initiated.) In the event the student declines the suggested referral, members are not obliged to continue the relationship.

6. Members adhere to the American College Personnel Association standards established in "The Use of Group Procedures in Higher Education: A Position Statement by ACPA," *Journal of College Student Personnel,* 1976, *17,* 161–168.

7. Members provide adequate orientation or information to students prior to and following any test administration so that the results of testing may be placed in proper perspective with other relevant factors. In so doing, members recognize the effects of socioeconomic, ethnic, and cultural factors on test scores.

8. Members inform students about the purpose of testing and make explicit the planned use of results prior to testing. Members ensure that instrument limitations

are not exceeded and that periodic review and/or retesting are made to prevent stereotyping.

9. Members recognize the limits of their competence in the administration, scoring, and interpretation of tests and perform only those functions for which they are qualified.

10. Members ensure strict test security because the meaningfulness of test results used in personnel, guidance, and counseling functions generally depends on students' familiarity with the specific items on the test.

11. Members do not permit the appropriation, reproduction, or modification of published tests or parts thereof without the expressed permission and adequate recognition of the original author or publisher.

12. Members refer to the following sources in the preparation, publication, and distribution of tests:
    a. *Standards for Educational and Psychological Tests and Manuals* (1974), revised edition, published by the American Psychological Association on behalf of itself, the American Educational Research Association, and the National Council on Measurement in Education.
    b. "The Responsible Use of Standardized Tests," the position statement of the American Association of Counseling and Development published in *Guidepost,* October 5, 1978.

APPENDIX 2.
National Association of Student Personnel Administrators Standards of Professional Practice

This statement was passed by the Board of Directors at the February 1983 meeting. The primary responsibility for the three-year evolution of the statement was managed by Dr. John Dalton of Iowa State University. It is presented here in its entirety.

Preamble

The National Association of Student Personnel Administrators (NASPA) is an organization of professional educators whose members represent colleges, universities and educational agencies by providing services that promote student educational and personal growth. The association seeks to promote student personnel work as a profession which requires personal integrity, belief in the dignity and worth of individuals, respect for individual differences, a commitment to service, and dedication to the development of individuals through education and personal growth. NASPA also seeks to support student personnel work through its efforts to expand professional knowledge and to provide opportunities for members to develop skills and expertise through professional education and experience. The following standards are endorsed by NASPA:

1. Professional Service

A member should provide professional service in a manner which fulfills the mission of the employing institution, and which supports the educational interests, rights and welfare of students.

2. Agreement with Institutional Goals, Mission

Members who accept employment with an educational institution imply agreement with the general mission and goals of the institution.

3. Management of Institutional Resources

Members seek to advance the welfare of the employing institution through accountability for the proper use of institutional funds, personnel, equipment, and other resources. Members inform appropriate officials of conditions which may be potentially disruptive or damaging to the institution's mission, personnel, and property.

4. Employment Contracts

Members honor employment contracts. Members do not commence new duties or obligations at another institution under a new contractual agreement until termination of an existing contract, unless mutually agreed to by the member and the member's current and new supervisor.

5. Conflict of Interest

A. Members recognize that their primary obligation is to the employing institution and seek to avoid private interests, obligation, and transactions which are, or even appear to be, in conflict of interest.

B. Members clearly distinguish between statements and actions which represent their own personal views and those which represent their employing institution when important to do so.

C. A member should reasonably restrict his/her private interest, obligations, and transactions to minimize the likelihood of conflict of interest or any appearance of impropriety.

6. Legal Authority

Members attempt to obey all lawful authority. Members refrain from conduct involving dishonesty, fraud, deceit and misrepresentation, or unlawful discrimination. NASPA recognizes that many legal questions are unclear, and members should seek the advice of counsel as appropriate. Members demonstrate concern for the legal and social codes and moral expectations of the communities in which they live and work even when the dictates of one's conscience may require behavior as a private citizen which is not in keeping with these codes/expectations.

7. Equal Consideration/Nondiscrimination

A. Members execute their professional responsibilities with fairness and impartiality and show equal consideration to individuals regardless of status or position.

B. Members encourage diversity and promote the educational and cultural advantages of pluralism.

8. Student Behavior

Members demonstrate and promote responsible behavior for students and support actions that enhance personal development of students.

Members seek to enhance the student's responsibility for his/her own behavior. In situations of threat to self, public health or safety, or of violations of law or institutional rules, regulations, or policies, constraints may be placed upon student behavior.

9. Accuracy and Integrity of Information

Members ensure that all information conveyed to students, employers, employees, supervisors, colleagues, and the public is factual and in appropriate context.

10. Confidentiality of Records

Members respect the confidential nature of education and professional records. Except where law requires, they shall disclose such information only with proper authorization.

11. Research Involving Subjects

Members are aware of and take responsibility for all pertinent ethical principles and institutional requirements when planning any research activity dealing with human subjects. (See *Ethical Principles in the Conduct of Research with Human Participants,* Washington, D.C.: American Psychological Association, 1973.)

12. Limitations on Professional Competence

Members define the nature and extent of their professional competencies when assisting students or others.

13. Hiring, Selection, Practices

Members support fair employment practices by broadly publicizing staff vacancies, selection criteria, and deadlines in accordance with established legal guidelines.

14. References, Judgments of Peers

Members provide accurate and complete information about candidates when serving as a reference including both relevant strengths and limitations of a professional and personal nature.

15. Job Definitions and Performance Evaluation

Members clearly define job requirements for employees and regularly evaluate their performance.

16. Work Climate; Cooperation

Members promote a work climate of mutual respect, trust, and collegiality.
Members work cooperatively with faculty and staff and with others outside the institution to promote institutional goals and programs.

17. Professional Development

Members have an obligation to continue personal professional growth by acquiring new knowledge, improving skills, sharing ideas and information, and participating in the meetings and affairs of the Association. Members encourage and facilitate the professional growth of staff whom they supervise and the development and improvement of the profession. Members emphasize ethical standards in professional preparation and development programs.

Index

A

Abelson, R., 20, 23, 27, 28
Administrators: and autonomy, 33-35, 38-39, 43; and ethical principles, 32-39, 43
Advisers, and ethical principles, 40
Ambler, D. A., 32, 47
American Association of Counseling and Development (AACD), 91, 96, 97; and allegations of violations, 61-62, 64; sanctions by, 62; standards of, 55, 56, 59
American Association of University Administrators (AAUA), 64; mediation by, 63; standards of, 56
American College Personnel Association (ACPA), 2, 28, 64, 83; ethical code of, 17, 18, 19, 22, 52, 53, 54, 55, 56, 57, 58, 59, 91-97
American Educational Research Association, 97
American Personnel and Guidance Association (APGA), 53, 55
American Psychological Association (APA), 46, 47, 60, 64, 94, 97, 100; enforcement processes of, 62; sanctions by, 62; standards of, 54, 55, 59, 61
Aristotle, 24
Association of College and University Housing Officers (ACUHO), standards of, 55, 59
Autonomy: and administrators, 33-35, 38-39, 43; and benefiting others, 23-24; and doing no harm, 22; and educators, 40-42, 43-44; and evaluators, 35, 39, 43; and faithfulness, 25; and organizer/coordinator, 34, 38-39; and planners, 32, 33, 36; principle of, 18, 20-21, 31; and resource managers, 33, 38; and staff development facilitator, 35, 39

B

Baier, K., 28
Balancing principle, and benefiting others, 23
Barr, P., 3
Baumgarten, E., 22, 27, 28
Beauchamp, T. L., 18, 19, 21, 22, 23, 25, 28
Benefiting others: and administrators, 33-35; and educators, 40-42, 44; and planners, 36-37; principle of, 22-24, 31
Benn, S. I., 24, 28
Bergin, A. E., 22, 28
Bok, D., 7, 15
Bowen, H. R., 68, 78
Brown, R., 3
Brown, R. D., 1-4, 32, 43, 46, 47, 67-87
Brubacker, J. S., 7, 15

C

Callis, R., 56, 60, 61, 64
Canon, H. J., 1-15, 17, 39, 47, 67, 78, 79, 81-87
Care, ethics of, 85-87
Careers as vocations, in ethical community, 73, 75
Carpenter, D. S., 64
Chambers, C. M., 21, 22, 26, 28
Chickering, A. W., 17, 28
Childress, J. F., 18, 19, 21, 22, 23, 25, 28
Churchill, L., 27, 28
Codes. *See* Standards
Colleagues: and adviser's sexual conduct, 10, 21, 22, 23, 27; and confidentiality, 9, 21, 24; and job counter offers, 10; and moving expenses, 10; workshop exercises of, 10, 22
Community, concept of, 70
Competence, and autonomy, 20-21
Confidentiality: and autonomy, 21; standards on, 100
Conflict of interest, standards on, 99-100
Conn, J. M., 79
Contracts, and faithfulness, 26
Council for the Advancement of Standards for Student Services/Development Programs, 53
Counseling, standards on, 96-97

D

Dagley, J. C., 3, 19, 49-65, 67, 75, 82, 83, 84, 85
Dalton, J., 99
Daniels, A. K., 50, 64
Decision making: model of ethical, 18; steps in, 50-51
DeCoster, D. A., 46, 47, 76, 78-79
Delworth, U., 3, 86, 87
DePauw, M. E., 64
Dolgoff, R., 50, 64
Donahue, J., 3
Drane, J. F., 18, 19, 28
Dutton, T. B., 36, 38, 47-48

E

Earth, as community, 71
Educators: and autonomy, 40-42, 43-44; and benefiting others, 40-42, 44; and doing no harm, 40-42, 44, 45-47; and ethical principles, 40-42, 43-45; and faithfulness, 40-42, 45; and justice, 40-42, 44
Employment and hiring, standards on, 93-94, 99, 101
Equality, and justice, 18, 24
Ethical community: agenda for, 69-72; analysis of creating, 67-79; careers as vocations in, 73, 75; checklist for, 72; humane learning environment in, 73, 77-78; and mission of student affairs, 68-69; need for, 78; peace and caring issues in, 72, 74; personal development in, 73, 75-76; planning for, 73-78; theory and research in, 73, 76-77; topics and program examples for, 72-73
Ethics: assumptions about, 1; barriers to inquiry on, 2-4; of care, 85-87; case examples of, 5-15; and colleagues, 9-10; committee role in, 83-84; community for, 67-79; and external constituencies, 14-15; feminine perspective on, 85-86; and generalizability, 28; in graduate student preparation cases, 6; hierarchy of reasoning on, 18; model for applying, 31-48; myths about, 81-85; and perfection, 82; as practical, 84; principles and decision making in, 17-29; rules of, 18-19; and special populations, 12-13; standards statements on, 49-65; and student development, 1-2; in student encounters, 7-8; and student organizations, 8-8; in supervisory relationships, 10-12; theory of, 28; thinking about, 81-87; and value clarification, 83; and value judgments, 82
Evaluators: and autonomy, 35, 39, 43; and ethical principles, 35
External constituencies: and conflict of interest, 14; and legislators' requests, 14-15, 22-23; and political candidacy, 14

F

Faithfulness: and administrators, 33-35; and educators, 40-42, 45; and planners, 37-38; principle of, 25-27, 32
Fargo, J. M., 19, 24, 29
Farmer, R. N., 37, 48
First Amendment rights, 8, 21, 82-83
Fischer, K. W., 29
Frankena, W. K., 21, 29
Fried, J., 3

G

Gilligan, C., 85-86, 87
Golann, S. E., 54, 64
Graduate students: attending to, 6, 25, 27; practicum supervisor for, 6, 22; seminar process group of, 6, 21; thesis research of, 6, 25, 26-27

H

Harm, doing no: and administrators, 33-35; and educators, 40-42, 44, 45-47; and instructor, 45; and mentor, 46-47; and planners, 36; principle of, 21-22, 31; and program planner, 45-46; and researcher, 46
Higher education, as community, 71
Hollander, P. A., 56, 63, 64
Humane learning environment, in ethical community, 73, 77-78
Hurst, J., 3-4

I

Impartiality, and justice, 24
Information, standards on, 100

Informed consent, and autonomy, 21
Institutional relationships, standards on, 93, 99
Instructors: and doing no harm, 45; and ethical principles, 40

J

Johnson, C., 4
Johnson, D., 2, 4
Justice: and administrators, 33-35; and educators, 40-42, 44; and planners, 37; principle of, 18, 24-25, 31-32

K

Kitchener, K. S., 3, 17-29, 31, 32, 43, 67, 78, 82, 84, 85
Kottler, J. A., 50, 65
Krager, L., 3, 31-48, 67, 78, 82, 85

L

Lambert, M. J., 22, 28
Legal authority, standards on, 100
Levinson, D. J., 46, 48
Loewenberg, F., 50, 64
Losito, W. F., 27-28, 29

M

Mable, P., 53, 64-65
McCaffrey, S. S., 49, 50, 65
McGowan, J. F., 50, 65
McKinley, D., 3, 4
Macklin, R., 20, 29
Mediation, and standards, 63
Mendenhall, W. R., 57, 65
Mentor: and doing no harm, 46-47; and ethical principles, 42
Mercy, J. A., 77, 79
Mill, J. S., 23
Miller, T. K., 53, 64-65
Moore, M., 4
Moore, W. E., 49, 65
Moral conscience, student services as, 68-69
Morrill, W., 4
Mueller, K. H., 51-52, 65

N

National Association of Student Personnel Administrators (NASPA), 65; standards of, 55, 56, 59, 99-101

National Association of Women Deans, Administrators, and Counselors (NAWDAC), 65; standards of, 54, 55, 56, 58-59
National Council on Measurement in Education, 97
Nielson, K., 20, 23, 27, 28
Noddings, N., 86, 87
Nolting, E., 3
Nondiscrimination, standards on, 94, 100
Nonmaleficence, principle of, 21-22

O

Organizer/coordinator: and autonomy, 34, 38-39; and ethical principles, 34

P

Paternalism, and benefiting others, 23
Peace Academy, 74
Peace and caring issues, in ethical community, 72, 74
Planners: and autonomy, 32, 33, 36; and benefiting others, 36-37; and doing no harm, 36; and ethical principles, 32, 33, 36-38; and faithfulness, 37-38; and justice, 37
Pope, S. K., 64
Powell, C. J., 20-21, 29
Principles, ethical: and administrators, 32-39, 43; and advisers, 40; analysis of, 19-27; of autonomy, 18, 20-21, 31; of benefiting others, 22-24, 31; conflict among, 32; described, 31-32; of doing no harm, 21-22, 31; of educators, 40-42, 43-45; and evaluators, 35; of faithfulness, 25-27, 32; of justice, 18, 24-25, 31-32; and mentors, 42; and organizers/coordinators, 34; and planners, 32, 33, 36-38; as prima facie valid, 27-28; and program planners, 41; and researchers, 41; and resource managers, 33; and staff development facilitator, 35
Professional preparation and development, standards on, 95-96, 100, 101
Professional relationships, standards on, 92-93, 101
Program planner: and doing no harm, 45-46; and ethical principles, 41

R

Ramsey, P., 25, 29
Rawls, J., 24, 29
Reciprocity, and justice, 24
Research: in ethical community, 73, 76-77; standards on, 94-95, 100
Researcher: and doing no harm, 46; and ethical principles, 41
Resource managers: and autonomy, 33, 38; and ethical principles, 33
Responsibilities, standards on, 91-92, 99
Rest, J., 29
Richman, B. M., 37, 48
Rickard, S. T., 36, 38, 47-48
Rissmeyer, P., 3
Rosenberg, M. L., 77, 79
Ross, W. D., 21, 23, 29
Rules. *See* Standards

S

Sanford, N., 1, 4
Schmidt, L. D., 50, 65
Schurr, G. M., 61, 65
Scott, W. R., 57, 58, 65
Seeman, D., 86, 87
Self-determination, and autonomy, 21
Smith, J. C., 79
Socrates, 22
Special populations: and affirmative action, 13, 25; and disability, 13, 25; and women, 12-13, 22, 25
Staff development facilitator: and autonomy, 35, 39; and ethical principles, 35
Standards: analysis of statements of, 49-65; for clarification of responsibilities, 51; comparisons of, 55; for conflict areas, 58-59; content of, 55, 56-57; contexts of, 49; contradictions among, 19; for decision making, 50-51; for ethical justification, 18-19; etiology of, 53-54; examples of, 91-101; limitations of, 59-60, 63-64; and mediation, 63; monitoring and enforcing, 60-63; for performance appraisal, 52-53; for protection of practitioners, 52; for protection of profession, 51-52; for public affirmation, 52; purposes and uses of, 50-53; role of, 83, 84-85; scope of, 54-56; for teaching, 50
Student development: in ethical community, 73, 75-76; and ethics, 1-2; and faithfulness, 26; and mission of student affairs, 68-69
Student organizations: and film censorship, 9, 22, 25; and gay/lesbian workshop, 9, 27; and investigative reporting, 8, 21, 22, 25; and residence director and resident, 8, 19, 27
Student services: areas of conflict in, 57-58; arenas and constituencies for, 5; bureaucratic setting of, 57-59; ethical principles and decision making in, 17-29; mission of, 68-69
Students: and disciplinary evidence, 7, 18, 20, 25, 27; and fraternity conduct, 7-8; standards on, 91, 100; therapy referral for, 7, 27
Supervision: and consulting business, 11; and gay/lesbian film, 11, 23; and staff challenge, 11-12, 23, 25; and staff input, 12, 22; and travel allowance, 11, 23

T

Taylor, P. W., 17, 29
Testing, standards on, 96-97
Tolsma, D. D., 79
Toulmin, S., 28, 29
Tripp, P., 4

U

United States, as community, 71

V

Van Hoose, W. H., 50, 65

W

Webb, W. B., 62, 65
Welty, J., 3
Wilensky, H. L., 49, 65
Winston, R. B., Jr., 3, 19, 49-65, 67, 75, 82, 83, 84, 85
Women: in daily practice case, 12-13, 22, 25; ethics viewed by, 85-86
Wright, D., 3